Poets From
Central England

Edited by Lynsey Hawkins

anch**or**books
Poetry by the People
for the People

anchorbooks

First published in Great Britain in 2006 by:
Anchor Books
Remus House
Coltsfoot Drive
Peterborough
PE2 9JX
Telephone: 01733 898102
Website: www.forwardpress.co.uk

SB ISBN 1 84418 446 3

Foreword

Anchor Books was established in 1992 to provide a platform for poets from all walks of life to showcase their poetry. Today, Anchor Books continues to provide an outlet for expression.

Poetry should be fun and, above all else, accessible to all. Anchor Books publications are for all lovers of traditional verse and of the art of rhyme, proving poetry doesn't have to be cryptic.

This regional poets collection, *Poets From Central England,* showcases delightfully the joy and inspiration we can all draw from where we live without even leaving the comfort of our own home.

Contents

The Poems

A Pot Of Gold

(To our darling granddaughter, Katherine)

I prayed and prayed for years and years, hoping that one day
That if I looked long enough at a rainbow, a pot of gold would come
my way
Rainbows came, and rainbows went
The years rolled on and on, and I began to fear that the pot of gold
had gone.
Then one lovely summer day, when the sun was in the sky,
The prayer that I had asked for came gently floating by,
It brought with it a baby girl, so beautiful to see,
Her little smile and her cry were all that were meant to be.
She is growing now, and with each day she fills my life with joy,
She wraps me around her little finger and always looks so coy.
But never mind she is worth it and my story will unfold,
You can guess what I call my granddaughter,
    My pot of gold.

Betty Ainscough (Doncaster)

The Kinky Woman

I'm the kinky woman,
I won't leave you alone,
Far from your side,
I never will roam.

Your *fine* scolding talking:
You *don't* want me! - a fact?
I'll ignore what you say
Take notice of that!

You set the standard so high?
You *don't* break of a law?
Never was so?
You *think* you are sure.

Your *wife* just divorced you:
I *want* this so agree,
You *split* with her
But you'll *not* split with *me!*

Dorothy Mary Allchin (Northampton)

Playing Games

You've let me down and not very gently
Thinking I was a fool for your love
You took my heart and tried breaking it in two
And as if that, for you, wasn't enough

You then tried to make me feel
Like I was the one here to blame
I never asked for you to love me
Yet you leave me to deal with the pain.

I think I know what the problem is here
You couldn't face the music and ran
I didn't deserve how you've left this though
On this occasion you didn't act a gentleman.

You made me feel like I'd done something wrong
Or is that just how I've perceived it here?
You never told me your intentions right from the start
So communication has not been very clear.

I have now moved on from asking the question
Of why you were playing games with me
It really wasn't doing me much good inside
Will I miss you? That's not very likely!

Louise Allen (Biggleswade)

Obese?

Went to the doctor's yesterday,
'Come in,' he said, 'it's a lovely day.'
'Good Lord,' he said, 'you're quite obese,'
Doctor I said I can easily see my knees.
He waddled back to his chair
Must have been 20 stone and a bit to spare,
He sat down and looked me in the eye,
Then proceeded to munch a large pork pie.
After that he took out his fags,
Lit up and took a very deep drag,
He said, 'What you need is more exercise,
Eat less food and get down a size.'
I left the surgery my brain in disarray,
Thinking tomorrow might be my very last day.
I've not been to the surgery for many a day,
Heard on the grapevine the good doctor had passed away,
I get on the scales, 12 stone it says,
When I walk past the doctors now, I give them a wave!

Don Antcliff (Derby)

Clouds

With a sense of wonder, I watch the clouds drift above the Earth,
Full of merriment and mirth.
At times swiftly with a fresh breeze they flow
Now white and fluffy, or be-smudged of grey, ever changing
Their performance and always re-arranging.
I visualise stately galleons of old, proudly sailing.
Often bold and haughty moods these clouds, never failing.

When summer skies bring perfect blue,
Quietly, small, white clouds may change their hue,
And loll around, maybe all day,
Enjoying basking in the sun's warm ray
Gently hovering, 'til the evening sky, tells dusk is nigh.
Then disappears from mortal eye:

As stormy weather takes on winter's clime,
Then clouds wear black, and thunder loud his chime
Darkens sky with winds of power that shriek
Chasing ever chasing, his to seek:
Yet winter will die, his fury lessening each day
For springtime brings her calmness into play.

Now drifting clouds commune with docile skies
Once more to court the summer sun, in merry guise
To flatter and tease with joyful motion
Filling each day with a magical potion,
Picturesque as ever, to mesmerise the eye
Against this wondrous world of ever widening sky:

Dorothy Athorn (Chesterfield)

You Are The Fragrance Of Today

A fleeting glance of a vision in pink
A floating walk of confidence
A glimpse of modern love
An emptiness that's left when you are gone
I follow, without delay
You are the fragrance of today.

I see your reflection in a mirror, as you pass with haste
Portraits hung along the wall
Where you stood and stared at them all
You departed down the stairs
Your perfume filled the air
But you are no longer there.

I waited impatiently by the door
I hoped you'd come back for more
I thought I saw your silhouette
And as I turn and run in hope
I breathe heavy as I pray
You are the fragrance of today.

Clive Atkins (Brackley)

Remembrance Day

The sky was grey and overcast,
The air peaceful and still.
The bitter cold mind-numbing
As I watched them from the hill.

They marched in lines, as always,
Their medals proudly worn,
You could sense the pride within them,
This regiment reborn.

Their sense of purpose evident,
To all, as they passed by,
Committed as they ever were,
To comrades doomed to die.

Folk huddled in the village square,
Those that had braved the weather,
The grey-stoned war memorial,
Where all would stand together.

At last they marched into the square,
And moved into their places,
Their heads were bowed, all silent,
And pain showed on their faces.

The hymns were sung, the readings read,
The vicar spoke with feeling,
The wreaths and poppies laid in place,
This was a time for healing.

Then I watched them as they moved away,
Another year gone by,
And as I walked down from the hill,
I brushed a tear from my eye.

K Ball (Wolverhampton)

The War Years

I was brought up in the War years,
When rationing was rife,
With not much on the table,
It was the bane of our life.

With dripping on the table,
With very little meat,
And clothing coupons in a book,
While others were used for sweets.

The rent man used to pay a call,
Whenever it was due,
Then Dad would go out rabbiting,
So we could have a stew.

We got goods on 'the weekly',
Like clothes and shoes alike,
We didn't own a motor car,
It was somebody's old bike.

But one way or the other,
We managed thro' the years,
Cos we were there for one another,
Throughout our troubles and our fears.

Brenda Barlow (Doncaster)

The Family

When the cares of the day are upon you
You feel you don't want to try
When the voices 'I want' all surround you
So tired you can't even cry
When the tasks you do seem unending
Your mind is saying - no more
When your body won't obey your instructions
And wants to lie down on the floor
Remember the ones who are lonely
No one needs their help through the day
No one needs their advice or a helping hand
No one listens to what they say
Then take a deep breath and say thank you
That you have so much to do
So many who love you and need you
When no one but Mum will do
For one day, the house will be silent
No one left to need your care
No voices raised and no laughter
No footsteps on the stair
But because of the love and attention
You have given throughout the years
They will come back to share with you
Their laughter, joy and tears
When you are feeling sad and lonely
Always - a knock and 'Hi Mum'
The house full of voices and laughter
And you - well you're back to square one.

Lydia Barnett (Nottingham)

A Mother's Love

She bears down to give birth,
To a son that takes her heart.
A new life is born on Earth,
And a love you cannot part.

She's as proud as she could be,
As she sings a lullaby song.
Her loves for all to see,
Her bond so incredibly strong.

Caring for him through his infant years,
And protecting him with all her might,
Wiping away his innocent tears,
And keeping him safe at night.

She tolerates his cantankerous ways,
And wipes his dirty nose,
Lapping up his childhood days,
While his curiosity grows.

Then comes the teenager from Hell,
With his temper ever flaring,
But she won't give up as she can tell,
He still needs her caring.

Her little boy is now a man,
And he's ready to fly the nest,
She knows she's done the best she can,
But still her heart won't rest.

She whispers the words, 'I love you,'
As she watches her young man leave,
She knows it's what he now must do,
But still she can't help but grieve.

A new beginning, a new life,
As he moves on to pastures new,
A first job, a beautiful wife,
But a mother who'll always love him too!

Diane Beamish (Cheltenham)

Fifty-Five

Fifty-five and still alive
No matter how I strive
So much still to give
Why do I not want to live?

Inside I feel so down
Trying not to frown
They have won you see
No longer am I me.

The more I try
I just want to cry
Holding it all inside
A scapegoat I want to find.

There is one I can see
Again it is me
Having done the crime
Must do the time.

How long must this go on?
For me this is no fun
Waiting for the end
What message does this send?

Garry Bedford (West Midlands)

Stranglehold

What purpose in life,
Has the ivy, that climbs,
Bringing death, to the trees of the woodland,
Whilst still in their prime?

What lesson can be learnt,
From the example it shows,
In its occupation of perfecting,
A crushing stranglehold.

Is it there - as a warning to all others,
Of what never should be,
The ability to use strength,
-     Quite needlessly.

With no respect for creation,
-     The continuance of life-
The 'ogre' of the woodlands
Carries the 'flag of death' with pride.

Taking away from others,
Who have never done it any harm,
Committing murder at will,
With an ever extending arm.

Richard Bennett (Bakewell)

The Four Seasons

Life comes back into the hedgerows
The blackbird sings his melodious tune
Hedgehogs stirred back into life by the sun and the moon.
Insecticide disrupts the balance which species is going to survive.
Only bent backs; and perseverance, the farmer his sickle and his
scythe.

Looking down across golden fields poppies swaying in the gentle
breeze
Rabbits in the corn constantly listening
While the planet is slowly being brought to its knees.
Milk fresh produce our luxury, all must be paid
Only with long hours and dedication, the farmer his fork and
his spade.

The field is half stubble the rest in furrows neatly laid down
A picture of the past and the future
The gulls overhead swooping the ground
The gift of the soil is mankind's provider
And only those who care for it know how,
Only hard work and endurance, the farmer his horse and his plough.

The landscape rests for tomorrow
Bulbs wait eagerly buried in the ground
The trees have all shed their plumage
More have been lost than been found.
Like vultures picking a helpless carcass
Very little for generations to come
Years of greed, in-breeding with selfishness
The faster we go, the faster we have to run.

J Bennetts (Burntwood)

Autumn Blues

Autumn is upon us
As summer quickly fades
The trees' green leaves are changing
To red and yellow shades.

The sun is not so warm now
The sky is not so blue
And birds don't sing as often
As they used to do.

A few brave flowers still grow
But most of them are dead
And the squirrel hoards a stack of nuts
Before taking to his bed.

Soon the winds will blow and snatch
The dead leaves from the trees
And these will make a soggy mess
Beneath the canopies.

The farmers' fields lie fallow
Where the earth is damp and dark
The nights are long, the days are short
No children in the park.

As the year moves slowly on
We know that all will change
For after autumn, winter comes
Then spring is here again.

Brenda Benton (Waltham Cross)

Gateway To The Countryside

Gateway to the countryside
A freedom so wide.
For the need of conservation
Welcomes England's colourful celebration.
That's shown in each county
Its own seasonal tapestry.
Where sleeping pastures
Turnover their textures.
That can live again
Seeking sunshine and rain.
Captured by a landscape painter
Its glory in watercolour.
For our nation to admire
But it's the countryside we desire.
Away from the working week
Just to hear nature speak.
While breathing in the pure fragrance
The clear air refreshes at an instance.
Along with friends or on my own
I still have to return home.

Alex Billington (Shefford)

The Asian Tsunami

(26th December 2004)

It came with awesome force 'tis said
As tiny babies lay in bed
Receding with ferocity
Soon washing them far out to sea
Those pleas for help and cries of pain
For most of them were all in vain
As everything around them fell
'Neath waves of water sent from Hell
At random; children wantonly
Were orphaned by the cruel sea
As mothers, fathers, families
And friends were claimed by Tsunami
Whilst tidal waves and earthquakes roared
Familiar sounds were all ignored
Until there lay on land and shore
One hundred thousand dead; and more
Sea water raged through tropic palms
As in the debris, legs and arms
Were bruised and beaten by the things
That tons of rushing water brings
Ships lay wrecked and boats destroyed
As buildings bent like celluloid
Then folded like a pack of cards
And drifted aimlessly towards
The open sea where people swam
In fear; some shouting here I am
A train is heard; a click; a clack
Then all lay still 'neath twisted track
Derailed and broken there it lay
So gone; two thousand lives, dare say
Where once a row of hotels stood
Idyllic scenes now heaps of wood
Mixed with concrete, steel and tin
Remains of everything within
Awash with mud and slimy sand
An epitaph untouched by hand
A battered car; a coach; a bike
Could all be seen; where ere you liked; to look

As flotsam everywhere
Caused all to weep and stand; and stare
First thoughts in minds midst everything
This surely can't be happening
What kind of demon thus awaits?
And with such force so devastates
As deadly as the atom bomb
Each kingdom went; to kingdom come
Now homeless in their millions wait
Confused as they evacuate
The villages and towns they knew
In which they prospered; loved; and grew
What now is life, to those who grieve?
No future can their minds perceive
Yet how they spur each other on
E'en though the zest for life has gone
No tragedy has ever been
So vile as this satanic scene
A happening not seen by man;
No never since the world began
As countries of the world donate
Fulfilling needs of those who wait
To help them gather threads of life
And comfort them in times of strife
Donations play their part alright
But cannot benefit the plight
Of those in trauma who live on
When all they loved in life has gone
Whilst Leery Budda idols rise
Triumphantly from their demise
And temples swathed in mire stand tall
In Holy guise above it all
The whole wide world will ne'er forget
That wild diluvial surge; and yet
Still; Sodom and Gomorra scoff
And sneer at nature's behemoth.

Maurice Ivor Birch (Walsall)

In The Eyes Of The Beholder

Don't gawk at me as if I am a freak,
Trapped in the arms of this mobile chair,
Cannot move nor speak.
Bones all gnarled and twisted,
Face misshapened by deep pain,
If your eyes cannot see what your eyes should see,
Then please don't look again.

Don't talk to me in baby ways,
For I am a full-grown child,
Trapped within a crumbling cage,
With my senses running wild.
Got no future, got no past,
Live each hour as if my last,
When I was born a spell was cast.
So little you know of me,
Yes, only what you see!

John Bilsland (Welwyn Garden City)

Winter White

Crisp and crackling, winter white!
Snow falling overnight!
Houses patterned by the dawn!
Sleeping people woke
And the second act of the play displayed
And nature once again
Has changed our lives.
It doesn't ask, it doesn't plan,
It doesn't just consider man!
This beautiful, terrible world!
It's kind and warm and clear and cold
It's very, very, very old.
Is it here to confuse man?
No! Just wrap up warm and understand
The snow that covers all the land
Is a wonderful, valuable gift!
You cannot wrap it, you cannot slap it!
It'll only change in it's own time,
No matter what you do, it's rare,
It's winter so it's there!

Joan Blissett (Kettering)

Shapes

Sometimes, a person's walk,
Will incline me to smile
Although I have no reason, because
I'd rather give a talk
Than allow anyone to see my style.

It's rather quaint, rich and beguiled
You can't register whether it's a saunter
Or if I'm breaking into a canter,
My legs are rather short
And my legs are peculiarly formed.
As if - someone forgot who I was to be
So now I'm totally transformed
Into a species never described before - or performed
Lots of people, hate, the way they are made
But I'll never be afraid
Although I resemble something by - De Sade.
Perhaps in the shape of things to come
From other planets - strangely dumb -
At least I'll know, I'm not the only one
Whose boots are two sizes, too big
As this allows my knees to buckle
If I'm carrying a scuttle.
In a marathon for people strangely shaped
If I go through mud I'll need a scrape.
So never forget, you that laugh,
You may rise tomorrow looking aghast
And run lopsided and not too fast
See - we from different planets
Have seen it all before, when we all looked like gannets.

A Boddison (Bridgnorth)

To Daffodils (Robert Herrick)

Fair daffodils, we weep to see
You haste away so soon;
As yet the early-rising sun
Has not attained his noon.

Golden trumpets herald us,
Heads nodding in the breeze,
Reminding me of warmth to come;
Forgetting winter's freeze.

If you could live, and never die,
Man's smile would linger on;
Melting memories that cause pain,
You sisters of the sun!

Diane Bowen (Birmingham)

More Than Pain

I think we were very close for a while,
You often made me smile.

I think we sort of sympathised
With all those really hurtful lies
That we were told throughout our years
And that we comforted with tears.

I thought we could endure the pain
That together we could stay sane
I would have stayed with you forever
I would have betrayed you never.

You didn't feel the same,
You thought it was a game.
You hurt me more than you could know,
You left me at the lowest low.

Was it worth it?
Did it make you happy for a bit?
To see me suffer as I did
The feelings that I had, I hide.

But I won't do that anymore
Because the love that you tore
Isn't worth my tears
I endured you for years.

Your hate, your spite, your stupid ways
And your silences for days.
I deserved so much more than you gave
I'd listen to you rant and rave.

I hope when you look at this, you grieve
Because your love I can leave
The truest loves are supposed to last forever
For years they will endeavour.

But now I know that you don't feel that way,
And I think it's just a crying shame, that you never thought to say.

Lucy Bradford (Stroud)

How Does Your Barley Grow?

When I see the spring barley so advanced for the season
I can barely now distance myself for this reason:
When my dear one had died leaving me all alone,
The time was near-soon for new seed to be sown.
But diverse all-rounders who took things in hand
Were either all scoundrels, or did not understand.
They said, 'Do not worry, there's much time till May'
When they should have said, 'Hurry! Start drilling today.'
No farmer delays sowing seed in his field,
For the sooner it's in, then the greater the yield;
And the former were seasoned, experienced men
So I've reason to think they knew better just then.
But I got it in sooner than they had intended
And withstood them bravely when they were offended.
They also laid plans for the sale of the farm
Which plans then afforded new cause for alarm;
For haymaking time would be well under way
And farmers reluctant to leave new-mown hay.
But I prayed, like Elijah, for plenteous rain
And God answered my prayer, yes, again and again.
The result was: my crops shot up healthy and strong,
And farmers came out to my sale in a throng.
Even so, to this day, though so many years on,
I think of the barley that nearly went wrong.

Edith Bright-Butler (Wantage)

Spirit Of The Fight

'Grandpa!'
'Yes' I said, perching him upon my knee,
Looking at his beaming smile,
His quizzing eyes held a question,
Was it going to be about me?
'Grandpa, back long ago, you had to go to war,
Why did you shoot, kill those men?
Was it that that made us poor?'
Offering him a biscuit, I thought, why was it so?
Remembering fallen comrades,
Tears welling: it wasn't show.
He stroked my face, frowning deep
He'd touched my memories deep,
I didn't know the answer,
Suppose I'll fathom it in sleep?
'Grandpa, sorry to make you cry,
Come on smile, you'll feel better then,'
Wiping tears; cuddling tightly,
This was now and that was then.
I'd told him tales of heroes,
How we'd fought side by side,
Dismissing the real horrors,
My medals were my pride.
It didn't mean a thing to him,
Why did we watch third light?
For masters safe on high ground,
Savouring battles bloody,
The spirit of our fight!

Josh Brittain (Mansfield)

For Those Who Remember

We all need a road we can walk down,
To a memory of long ago,
And a time where we shared in the passing,
In a war that the old only know.
For there in the past lies a lifetime,
A face or a place lingers on,
So real one can reach out and touch it,
Reliving each moment that's gone.
And was it a village in Belgium?
Girls laughter caught on the air,
Or was it that push up the Rhineland?
And the scenes then of utter despair,
Remembering all of your comrades,
And the stories that each had to tell,
Of the pubs that they sang and they drank in,
And the marching and fighting through Hell.
And the medals the old proudly wear now,
Heroes were they one and all,
And they look down those years tinged with sadness,
When youth proudly answered the call.
Judge not then today's generation,
For lessons that's never been learned,
For you can't tell how hot is the furnace,
Till the tips of your fingers are burnt.
And as the sun rises each morning,
Setting to herald each night,
So the watchers shall hide in the shadows,
As the lights on the highway shine bright.
And the doers will always burn bridges,
Chasing truth that is not always there,
For a question can have many answers,
While not all of the answers are fair.
To the lovers then, leave them the night time,
Let the dreamers dream while they may,
The young have today and tomorrow
To the old folk belongs yesterday.

J Brohee (Richmond)

Beautiful

Your smile is beautiful
As the new day's sun,
Warming us inside
With new strength to go on.

Your hands are beautiful
Holding gently, yet firm,
More comforting and safe
Than the taste of new wine.

Your voice is beautiful
Telling stories of grace,
Words giving life
When life's hard to face.

Your feet are beautiful
Leading us where,
We can dance on the
Seashore as if without care.

Your creation is beautiful
Skies, seas and flowers,
Your gifts of beauty
Forever are ours.

Dorothy Brooks (Sheffield)

The World Is Fine

All at once the world is fine,
Because you are completely mine, the
Stars shine brightly up above,
To prove how great this thing called love.

Each day seems to bring new happiness,
My cares seem to matter less and less,
So darling now you surely see, just
How much you've done for me.

The world is such a wonderful place,
When I look upon your familiar face,
Nothing matters any longer, as my love
For you grows ever stronger.

Ted Brookes (Doncaster)

Sheep In The Country

A ride in the country,
The sheep are grazing,
Eating the grass,
While the cars go past,
The restful, gaze,
As we go through,
The maze, the,
Scenery, so lovely,
Time to leave,
To weave through,
The trees.

B Brown (Chesterfield)

Down The River Of Dreams

The winding river wends her way
Down to the waiting sea
Past meadows of our childhood dreams
Now just a memory.

Those childhood days of make-believes
And once-upon-a-times
Beside the river of our dreams
Our hearts with love entwined.

But somehow things weren't meant to be
And to the waiting sea
Down the river of our dreams
You sailed away from me.

Malcolm Wilson Bucknall

One Wish

Remember the famous Christmas story
When Christ was born, 'neath a star of glory,
Twinkling and gleaming it shone from afar,
Beaming down through the night, a Christmas messenger star.
Attracting shepherds in fields, with its brilliant light,
An angel vision followed appearing so bright,
Gave a wonderful message of a newborn king,
Peace and goodwill to all men, he would bring.
Rejoicing they travelled following the Christmas star,
Met three wise men too, who had travelled afar,
In an inn's humble stable, Jesus they eventually did discover,
Surrounded by mooing animals, Joseph and Mary his mother,
Special gifts were offered to Jesus by each one -
Before leaving to spread the good news to everyone!
This Christmas star shines in our hearts each year.
Reborn is the Christmas message of peace, goodwill and cheer.
Gifts and Christmas cheer spread the message to all,
Gathering a momentum like a gigantic rolling snowball,
'Merry Christmas' lights and banners sway in the breeze,
Welcoming city shoppers and excited children they please.
Charities everywhere reach out, to all those in need,
Especially foreign countries, urgent help they plead,
If I had *one wish* that wish would surely be
That together the whole wide world would live peacefully,
Learning to understand and love one another,
Releasing anger and fear and act as a brother.
May this Christmas star of glory keep shining all around,
Not just at Christmastime but each day be found.
I wonder do you share this *wish* with me?
No guns, bombs, wars, a miracle it would be!

S Bush-Payne (Birmingham)

A Country Lane In Winter

When the leaf is withered
And the fruit devoured,
There is only the bare,
Forbidding branch
Against the sky.

The strangled wish
Lies like a broken stalk
In the dead field,
Stripped of harvest,
Empty of seed.

The midnight branches
Groan with the wind
In angry supplication,
While black clouds
Smother the moon.

Nothing can heal the wound,
Neither the dark,
Nor rhapsody of stars,
Nor Orphean melody,
Nor angel's song.

Dorothy Buyers (Oswestry)

The Push

They died in the boats,
They died in the water,
And on the beach,
And in the air.
They died and kept on dying,
On D-Day, over there.
Men pouring forth
Like water into sand.
Being used up,
Mopping up,
The machine gun fire from land.
Hacked and blasted.
Torn and broken,
In this push to gain the upper hand.
So many dead.
So many scarred inside and out.
Soldiers high on fear and adrenaline.
Of that there is no doubt.
They fought, they killed,
Stabbed and shot and tore.
The life we have now
Must justify
That savagery of war.

Miki Byrne (Birmingham)

When The Poppies Fall I Remember

I remember one September when I was just fourteen
Everything white was camouflaged to different shades of green,
Children were evacuated to different country places
They were sad to leave and arrived with tear-stained faces,
I remember cheering the forces as they looked so smart
Our young minds didn't realise what horror was to start.
I remember food and clothes all went on the ration
Land girls were brought in to help feed the nation.
I remember the Americans, Anzacs, Canadians and Gurkhas from
                                                        Nepal,
And all the men and women who answered the Nation's call.
I remember Eisenhower, Montgomery, Churchill and Chamberlain
And Vera Lynn singing, 'We'll Meet Again'.
I remember the Desert Rats, the brave Burma men
The black-out, the buzz bombs, and ARP wardens.
And I remember Dunkirk, the Battle of Britain too,
The droning of the bombers, as on their way they flew.
Sirens wailing, guns firing, waiting for the all clear
And the never-ending convoys when D-Day was drawing near.
I remember GI brides, prefabs and Nissen huts
And utility furniture that didn't cost too much.
I remember the weary prisoners arriving home at last
Without any counselling they had to forget the past.
I remember VE Day the people all went wild,
The King and Queen waved from the balcony, not everybody smiled.
For no one is a winner when fighting a war
Both sides lost people they loved and cared for.
When the poppies fall in the Albert Hall,
I remember them all
For they gave the most precious gift they could give
They gave their lives so that we might live.

Mollie Carter (Burton-on-Trent)

Save A Little Love

Save a little love in your heart
Keep the fondness in your smile
Let not parting give tears a start,
Savour the memory for a while.

Then offer up your hand sweet maid
That I may take it, and hold it to me,
Tenderness of your touch is all need said.
Love as faithful as ours, lasts for eternity.

Walk along life's pathway of friendship
Then gifts you will bestow, will in memory dwell.
There in silent affirmation a smile of fellowship
Shines out to say, my love I give for all pain to quell.

John Clarke (Gloucester)

My Dad

When I think of my dad, I think of the time
When I was quite small, he was strict, but that's fine.
He worked so hard to care for us all,
Long hours were the norm and always on call.

We would wait on the corner for him to appear,
And run up the street, our tales he would hear.
Fridays were special, he would call in the shop
And buy penny ice lollies, when the weather was hot.

We would polish his shoes, but took it in turns
On inspection a packet of sweets we could earn.
On special occasions we all had a treat,
A packet of crisps and some chocolate to eat.

We had an old banger and on picnics we went,
We would play in the fields till our energy spent.
At dusk we would pack up and home we would go,
Tucked up in blankets, no heater as so.

One night we were naughty and had all gone to bed
We were tissing up the wall when a loud voice said,
'You are bad children,' and he smacked all our bums,
It didn't hurt really, but it quietened us some.

As he went down the stairs, we pretended to cry
And looked at our bottoms for pink marks to compare.
Only one smack can I ever remember,
So that night we were bad to receive a good sender.

When I look back my memories of Dad are so precious,
Because when I was eleven, he died and left us.
So if you have a dad and you love him real good,
Tell him so - now, because I wish I still could.

I still miss you Dad.

Dorothy-Ann Cluley (Sileby)

The Silent Brave Army (The Misses And Mums Of Britain)

They come and go, quick, fast and slow.
Always there, always ready to go
They never fail or doubt or falter,
Always the same they never alter.
Ready to help, ready to give,
Happy all day giving to live.
No medals, no praise, they do not need
Willing to follow the right kind of lead
The children grown and flown
The struggle, mortgage now they own
Some to manage on their own
To sleep in a house by oneself
Takes courage not bought off the shelf
To show a brave face in morning light
Not to lose heart, put things right.
Learning to fix a plug or fuse
Getting used to help refused
To do things oneself is always the best
What's left undone, God helps with the rest
When each day's work is over they return
To an empty house but they're not alone
For God is in their hearts and in their home
They always give thanks for what they receive
For that is their faith, that is what they believe
To do without, is no sacrifice
'Make do and mend' have half a slice
Yes! When the battle's over and done
You'll find them still on the run
Jumbles cake stalls, knitting stalls
And most important work of all
There they are in church on Sunday still,
Praying for strength just to do His will
God bless the misses and mums of Britain
Come on chaps! Give them three cheers!
What would we do without them?

Millicent Colwell (St Albans)

Words

Unclench your hands
Put your arms down
I have come to talk,
Not roll around.
Say your words
I will say mine
We will come to a compromise
We will make it fine.
If one wants more
Things might not work.
When this happens,
People get hurt.

K Cook (Luton)

The Blind To See

Jesus help me to see
The good in others
As they in me
To open our eyes
To this beautiful land
Help people to see
With Your guiding hand.

I Corbett (Rugeley)

Growing Up

I've forgotten childish dreams; now I'm in an adult world
Time to face the facts - harsh reality uncurled
Changing all that I'd believed
That crazy, selfish, senseless greed
Recreate a vision; accept this is real world.

The hands of time cannot be turned; self-blame is no solution
To live and learn and act, there's no time for retribution
Mistakes I may have made
But the price has now been paid
Time to let go of the past - with - no more mind pollution.

Diane Crouch (Flitwick)

Eternal Love

You came to me
    Like a whisper in the night,
From your other world
    And told me of your love.

Watch the petals of a rose
    Unfolding in the sun
You will find my love
    In the sweet scent.

Watch the crystal waterfall
    Sparkle and glisten
As it dances over the rocks.
    Open your heart and listen
To the music of my love.

Watch the wonder of the rainbow
    As it spans your world and mine.
See the glowing colours
    And read the message of my heart.

With the swirling mists
    I will embrace you.
With the jewelled stars
    I will light your way.

Like the night
    I will surround you
In a velvet cloak of love
    And for all eternity
I will protect you.

Then, when the angel of light
    Wraps you in his silver wings
And brings you back to me
    I will take your hand in mine.

Together at last we will sing
      The symphony of our love.
Like a blazing comet it will fly
      Across the mystic universe.

There forever to shine in glory
      To bear witness to our story
How the power of true love
      Transcends beyond all reason
The boundaries of Earth and Heaven.

Brigitta D'Arcy-Hays (Olney)

Contrasts In Two Worlds

The cuckoo calls float clear on the still evening air
Like the church bells dying notes that gently fade away
England's green and pleasant country remains so fair
Quiet and peaceful on that lazy summer's day.

While far away in Flanders, soldiers lie in trenches
Exhausted by the battles they collapse in sleep
Soon they'll be 'over the top' to make advances
Many will be brave, some afraid and some will weep.

A gurgling brook runs merrily through woods day by day
And wild birds come calling to sing their sweet songs
While the sound of laughter rings from children at play
Happy, innocent and carefree all the day long.

Dawn breaks on the western front to light a vast scene
A shell pocked land of trenches all of which are bare
Mud lies everywhere without a sign of green
Churned by countless bombs and shells dealt without a care.

What a contrast between those two distant places
Why were the young sacrificed what was the fighting for?
A temporary piece of land or a sea of mud
The losses just illustrate the folly of war.

Terry Daley (Rugby)

The One I Love

You are the one I truly love,
You make my heart flutter like a dove.
I will be with you for evermore,
This I do know for sure.

When you came into my life,
I knew I wanted to be your wife.
I knew from the very start,
We would be together till death do us part.

I love you darling, oh so much,
I love to feel your gentle touch.
It makes me happy just to say,
My love grows more in every way.

D Dickens (Wellingborough)

Captured Silence

How still the air, how still the breeze,
How still the flowers, how still the leaves,
No creak of tree, no snap of twig,
No lap of waves from yonder brig,
No cry of gull from chimney pot,
No call of crow from garden plot,
How still the air.

No song of bird, no buzz of bee,
No whir of fly, no fly to see,
No bark of dog, no howl of cat,
No squeak or scratch of mouse or rat,
How still the air.

No gentle rap on windowpane,
No pattering sound of summer rain,
No heavy tread on kitchen floor,
No one knocking at the door,
How still the air.

No shriek or scream from children small,
No older ones chasing ball,
No idle chat from friendly neighbour,
Now at rest from daily labour
How still the air.

How still the air, how still am I,
In this wondrous peace I lie,
For in my heart and in my mind,
I am at one with all mankind,
One with all that lives on Earth,
One with God who gave me birth,
How still am I.

Mabel Dickinson (Leeds)

Untitled

Look for the sunshine all the time
Look for the goodness not the grime
Look for the smile, the helping hand
Let not the dark get the upper hand
Look for the happiness and the grin
Look for the kindness and the caring
In all of your life look for the good
Let it soak in your being
And change your mood
Don't let the Devil have his way
Beat off those clouds which are so grey
Think happy, be happy, share it always
Pass happiness on, make it a craze
Spread it like butter, thick and rich
Let it start with you then thoroughly mix
Amongst those you love and those you know
And just watch everyone glow.

M Dobbs (Leeds)

Hearts Of Love And Hate

God gave life to each newborn
He used His breath to fill their lungs
A strong loud cry says I am here
'Twas the miracle of love from God.

Millions like these breathe the same breath
They grew into young men races all
The hearts of some grew cold and cruel
Full of hate for those with soft hearts.

They gathered together waging war,
Determined to take everyone's land
Good men died - leaving loved ones behind
God did not give His breath for this.

A beautiful world green land blue skies
Scented flowers perfume pure.
Scenery like Heaven itself
Yet these evil men devour all.

War after war they knew not love,
They wave their slogans of hate and fear,
While soft hearted men pray for peace,
The evil minds just think to kill.

Years of suffering, years of war
A miracle from God's right hand will be,
To soften hearts of evil men,
Wars must end - tears must end.

Rosina M Drury (Dunstable)

Retirement

I used to dream of retirement,
Living a life of leisure,
Anticipating years to relax,
Thoughts that gave me pleasure.
But when the time came,
Nothing worked out to plan!
A widow, everything to do,
So much of which needed a man!
OK I can cope, I thought,
With all life can throw at me!
I'm resourceful! I'll get on alone,
Tho' busier than ever I used to be!
Strangely, it seems
I enjoy, these responsibilities!
A new confidence, is mine,
Despite bodily disabilities!
Some days are fraught!
But all problems can be solved,
There's a way around everything somehow!
People are kind, when you grow old!
Pocketing pride, you ask for help,
If things go wrong you laugh at yourself!
It's a new phase of life, make it work for you,
Enjoy your 'retirement' there's so much to do!

E Eagle (Malvern)

Truth To Tell

To you I have a truth to tell
Of feelings that will remain true
The way I feel and will always love you
From the day I met you, to when I pass away
My love for you will never stray
I also know you feel the same
Sometimes I think you believe it all a game
I believe you're scared, which is to blame
Now face up to it and call my name
We were together a long time before
The hurt and pain isn't no more
As I still love you as I did before
I know you love me, and that I'm sure
It would be weird to try it all again
But I'm certain our love would last to the end
So now open up to me and no longer pretend.

Kelly Earnshaw (Pontefract)

Weather Watch

The clerk of the weather said, Oh,
I've slipped up on the months, oh no!
For January brings the snow
And makes their feet and fingers glow:
Then February brings the rain
To thaw our frozen lakes again.
They'll blame the Government for this
And greet the PM with a hiss.

The experts said that they would see
A blackest winter there could be,
But now no rain, no rivers fill -
A hosepipe ban and summer ill.
I'll have to speak to God instead
That they may have their daily bread!

Owen Edwards (St Albans)

Nightlife

The midnight cloak surrounds me.
I feel a chilling breeze.
There is rustling in the bushes
Then I hear a hedgehog sneeze.

The hedgehog just ignores me,
As he trundles on his way.
He grunts and snuffles noisily,
In his constant search for prey.

I love the serenity of night,
As daytime mortals sleep.
Then the secret, silent nightlife
Out from all places, creep.

Unseen trees and whispering wind,
Quiet my mind, as I watch
Out of the hedgerow, the shadowy form
Of a furtive and wary young fox.

My senses whet, as I sit here,
In the pitch black starry night.
I hear the softly trodden deer,
Its grace is my delight.

Mouse scurries, darting forth,
She's always in a hurry.
I expect with all those mouths to feed,
It must be such a worry.

An owl screeches overhead,
Sounds eerie, blood-curdling,
Electrified senses so alive,
Clandestine life, pulsating.

Karen Fedrick (Didcot)

God's Gift

Out in the garden on a warm summer's day
My flowers are out in full display.
Fruits on the trees are growing well,
The apples I watch and see them swell.
Runner beans with long tender pods,
Satisfaction I give them a nod.
Carrots are long with roots so pink
Gallons of water they do drink.
Cabbages are a bright deep green,
Buzz of a bee is she the queen.
Yes the onions what a surprise
They only bring tears to your eyes.
Potatoes will follow on late
Peeling them is a job I hate.
Cinderella's pumpkin is ready to go
With tender hands I helped to grow.
See my beetroot in smart red jacket
I just followed the instructions on the packet.
With slugs and worms, beetles too,
Too many to mention but just a few.
So look around it's plain to see
There's food for the birds and food for me.

E Fensome (Luton)

Ending

Sky is challenging
Sunny last moments of the day,
Dying like a seascape in fog;
Shadows lurk incisively,
Breezes sleeping with daylight's dimming,
As dusk troubles tentative infiltration,
And urges meditation;
Frittering near, a wind swirls,
And my hair curls as though touched
By caressing hands,
My mind furls its sails
Like a boatman returning to port,
And bails out its frail cargo.

I am slipping towards sleep -
Scattering into unconsciousness
Seeing within where I am.

Juliet Fowler (Brampton)

Autumn

How wonderful to see all the pretty colours displayed,
The good Lord changes all of them completely without our aid.
The reds and yellows the greens and brown,
The good Lord really goes to town.

Nature is a wonderful thing,
Watch all the colours that autumn can bring.
The good Lord's hand is at the helm,
Gazing at autumn, can really overwhelm.

The squirrels are gathering in the nuts,
The hedgehogs are looking for safe holes, not ruts.
The leaves they will gather as they fall from the trees.
To make their soft beds where they can sleep with ease.

Very soon now winter will be here.
If the snow is very thick the children will cheer.
But let's think of the animals are they warm enough,
With the good Lord's care they will see it through,
Even though winter may be rough.

Zoe French (Birmingham)

Your Perfume

What is this aroma, this perfume?
So adorning, which fills this room
Such a sweet fragrance that fills
My head with its delightful thrills
Is it I wonder the aroma of a rose
Or more, a consciousness you impose
That you are near, when you are not
Stirring thoughts and passions hot
'O' sweet fragrance that alone is yours
Giving reason my heart to race without pause
Times together spent long have past
Yet your perfume's passion lingers to last
Return soon my sweet fragrant maid
That your beauty my mind not fade
My respect for you holds back with care
Yet youth in me cries out with passionate flare
With overwhelming passion my body blooms
To be wrapped in your naked bodies perfume
Our arms to entwine in sweet embrace
My hands quivering your form to trace
'O' that sweet fragrance of your perfume
With our sighs of loving filling a room
This, with your perfume, I have missed
Take me kiss these lips that have long not kissed
This, when I am alone with your fragrant scent
Is how my mind for your passion is sent.

James E Friday (Loughborough)

I Love You

When you look at me, and I look at you
With ruby lips and eyes of blue
What can it be between you and me?
That we enjoy each other's company.

Is it the flowers that bloom, or the birds that sing
Or is it the fact, that it is spring
That we feel and act the way we do
Then whisper to each other, 'I love you.'

T Gibson (Leicester)

Footprints In The Sand

They stumbled up the beach with rifles in their hand
Completely unaware of their footprints in the sand.
Bodies of their comrades were strewn along the shore
Some they'd known forever, others just a week or more.

The echoes of the *ack ack* gun firing overhead
The steady surging forward adding to the dead
Yet inch by inch they battled making fast a stand
Onward ever onward went the footprints in the sand.

A sense of jubilation as they gained a little ground
The sweet smell of victory above the battle sound
Each man knew his duty in this alien foreign land
And God left His footprints besides theirs in the sand.

This was a fight for freedom not for themselves alone
But sisters, wives and mothers left behind at home.
When the war was over and peace came to the land,
Only ghostly figures left footprints in the sand.

Joan Gallen (Redditch)

My Garden

Sweet smells of success from my garden I do grow
With flowers all around me from seeds I did sow
A recipe for happiness that is true for me
How I love my garden, a wonderful place for me
Oh how I love my garden, a place I long to be
With flowers all around me paradise I see
A haven of colour, a wonderful sight
The birds eating nuts from morning till night
The berries glistening in the sun on the holly tree
The blackbird singing so happily
Now the rain is falling the flowers look so clean and so bright
Almost dancing with sheer delight
To feel the rain on their petals is sure to make them strong
Now I hear the blackbird singing his song
He must be so happy, he feels so free
Living in my garden in the laurel tree.

Kath Gay (Whitwick)

Wake Up England

England, oh my England, I remember when came through war
Much battered but proud of what we had achieved,
Our heads held high but tinged with silent memories of those for
        whom we grieved,
Our Navy whose ships stretched as far as the eye could see,
Tempered in the heat of battle to keep us free.
An Air Force whose aircraft filled the skies a thousand at a time,
And our Army who fought for us worldwide.
Also an Empire, of which some today think was to our lasting shame
But to me a thing of pride, a great achievement of this nation,
This old England in her glory days.
What was to come in from the nineteen fifties on - what was
        to come?
Then it was said that this old England was tired out and broke.
The nation's workers wanted change and some a revolution.
They wrecked our great industrial might,
Our Empire, given up piece by precious piece, till nought was left
        except a Commonwealth.
We were descending into night.
In nineteen seventy-two the Government signed half our powers
away to join a so-called Common Market with wonderful free trade
To find that we were sucked further and further in,
Like water down a drain, losing our precious freedom bit by precious
        bit,
But this nation hasn't woken yet.
We walk as if asleep, unconscious of our fate.
The EU want this England divided into regions, the name of this great
Country will exist no more.
Why did we fight for freedom through that long and bloody war?
If as a nation we finally awake God forbid that it is not too late.

Howard Gibbs (Marlborough)

The Big C

So now it's said, that word whirls round inside my head.
I am immobilised, can't speak, and you just stare at me and seek,
Some reassurance that this can't be true.
Fate could not play this cruel trick on you
Oh! These are words we never thought to hear,
My eyes meets yours, which are so full of fear.
I rush to hold you in my arms, as I have always done.
When faced with life's big challenges.
We're going to win this one.
Though warned the going will be tough
Our love will see us through.
Not even the Big C will break the bond of me and you.

M Goodchild (Aylesbury)

The Memory Of Happiness

Those happy times we don't forget
When we were young and bold,
Those carefree days seem long ago,
Now we are growing old.

Those passing years of schooldays,
The friendships that we had,
Friends not seen, but thought about
With happy memories to make us glad.

And then came along the only one,
Our soulmate and we knew
That this one was our destiny
With a love so strong and true.

Children brought more happiness,
With loving memories to share,
The laughter and such happy times,
And life seemed always fair.

Through time we had our ups and downs,
The illness and the strife,
And the death of dear ones close to us,
In the tapestry of life.

But happy memories are many more
Than the sad ones in our lives,
We never forget those dear ones
In our hearts where they abide.

But sorrow fades and becomes more manageable
As each day follows day
And the memory of happiness
Is in our lives to stay.

Joan Gorton (Pontefract)

Springtime

There are crocuses and daffodils,
The cold wind of winter left and gone,
A gentle breeze to take its place
A meadow full of buttercups.
The sun to warm our hands and face,
Bluebells in the woods of green,
The most beautiful sight that's ever seen
Is springtime in all its shades of green.

Yvonne Golledge (Luton)

Mountain Rose

High up on the mountain top
A volcano weeps her lava of joy,
Two people joined in matrimony.

Confetti blows in the wind of love,
Doves fly high up to the mountain top.
Love will bind you together,
To walk down the path of love forever.

Hush . . . Listen to the word of love,
To the echoes within,
Where happiness belongs,
And souls unite.

She sweeps her hair from her lovely face,
And amazes him with her grace.
And so their vows are said.

Years pass by . . .
And white roses shall wilt.
But their joy remains,
And their love will blow like petals from the mountain top.

Paula Greaves (Bromyard)

Some Things . . .

Some things are just too easy to say,
And some things lie hidden, in wait for the day,
Some things are things that are meant for the night,
And some things are peaceful and loving and light;
Some things are spontaneous with no thought at all,
And some things are whispered, a quiet way to call,
Now some things are actions speak louder than words,
Like some things to do with the bees and the birds;
But there's something so beautiful mere words can't express,
And it's something about you I love nonetheless,
It's something so wond'rous I could just keep on going,
Describing that something you're already knowing;
Now some things are quiet, without any doubt,
And some things are silent, and try to get out;
But some things just scream 'cause they want to be heard
As something that sounds like the unspoken word.

Andy Gresty (Banbury)

You're Not Old

As we are getting older,
Our bones begin to creak,
And grey hair starts a showing
So our hearts begin to sink
But we are in our prime
Our life has just begun
So buck up, dress up, put on your face
Get out there and have some fun.

We may not be getting younger
But that doesn't mean to say
That life has passed us as it travels on its way
So take the pills and potions
That keep us at our best
Take out those shoes and handbag
And put on your favourite dress
We may be slightly larger
Than we were a year ago
It only keeps us warmer, in the winter, didn't you know
Believe that we are in our prime
Our life has just begun,
So buck up, dress up, put on your face
Get out there and have some fun.

Renalta Hall (Rushden)

The Weather

The weather is big news in our age
Talked about in every newspapers page!
Some people get worried by the weather,
We can be prepared for it, we cannot tether.
It affects all people in our world today
We see pictures on TV of hurricanes and earthquakes far away.
In Britain or Europe, it is mostly floods we expect,
Heavy storms or perhaps a tornado is the most that we get!
We hope for a good community spirit today
To help those in need in our own region or countries far away.
We never know if it will be our turn next
To be in a position of peril we do not expect.
We can only do our best with the weather
Simply 'grin and bear it' and pull together
The weather forecasters help us to prepare
In our own country or places afar!
A worldwide problem we have to cope with
A lifelong problem wherever we live!

Joyce Hallifield (Swadlincote)

Swim Fit

I disappointed Tom and Harry
When they walked upon this Earth
As I couldn't swim at all.

Tom swam well and Harry better
He swam St Lawrence river
Yet I couldn't swim at all.

I was frightened of all water
The sea was large and cold
The waves a source of terror
When I couldn't swim at all.

Many people tried to teach me
The best I did was float,
Still I couldn't swim at all.

Now eighty-six all that has changed
Club Otters I have joined
A caring club with coaches
Succeed where others failed.
I now can swim some more.

So thank you to those 'Otters'
From me and those gone aft
I too can now enjoy a swim
Tom and Harry may rejoice.

Dolly Harmer (Leighton Buzzard)

The Five Senses Of Love

What is this thing called Love?
You cannot feel it, yet it has a touch.
So gentle yet strong,
You feel you belong.

What is this thing called Love?
You cannot smell it, yet you know it's there
It's in the air, it's everywhere.

What is this thing called Love?
You cannot taste it, yet it has a flavour
We all love to savour
Sweet or sour, it still has power.

What is this thing called Love?
You cannot hear it
Yet it's loud and clear
Music to the ear.
Heartbeats are heard, like the song of a bird.

What is this thing called Love?
You cannot see it yet it has a hold.
On young and old,
On rich or poor for evermore.

Nancy Harris (Northampton)

Keep On Smiling

Let me hold you up
If you think you may fall
I can be your shoulder to lean on
The steady hand that reaches out
The eyes that have the wisdom when to listen
You have shown me how precious life is
How to hold my head up high
Stand tall and proud in the faces of those
Who try to bring us down
Even when I still feel a sense of shame
You are there, my friend, my guide
You keep me safe from my own fears
And the darkness that threatens at times to envelop me
My feelings of rejection are no longer there
As you wipe away my tears
You encourage me to embrace the future
To keep smiling through the clouds of doubt
Because of you I see more clearly
Together we can face the shadows
That may darken our paths
And revel in the good times
That are yet to come to light
But are just around the corner.

Michelle Harvey (Milton Keynes)

Tom, Dick And Harry

Tom, Dick and Harry, just to name a few,
Were ordinary people, just like me and you.
They joined a band of volunteers to fight a looming foe,
But did they think of dying when into battle they did go?

Up in the sky, upon the sea, the trenches far away,
Heading for that moment, the battle of D-Day.
They volunteered for fighting, with chance that they may die,
Just like the Spitfire pilots in their battles in the sky.

I cannot see the difference, in the air, on land or sea,
These volunteers were out there, for themselves and you and me.
Their efforts put together, whether large or small,
Put together something, a message to us all.

Tom and Dick and Harry, Ed and Frank and Hugh,
And ordinary citizens, were all part of the 'few'.
Monuments are memories, that is what they're for
Just like the kneeling miner who kneels on Dover's shore.

He played his part way down below as diamonds he did mine,
His battles he fought bravely for that was his front line.
Bevin boys were soldiers, perhaps you did not know,
A number, drawn at random, said to war they could not go.

It's the way the cookie crumbles, when you have no choice,
Stuck where you don't want to be because you have no voice.
We are all Tom, Dick and Harry, Vera Lynn and Sue,
We played our part quite willingly, but are thankful for the 'few'.

R Harvey (Nottingham)

Angels On Earth

Angels enter in our lives, disguised in many ways,
Believe it or believe it not, there are those special days.

I've met some angels in my life, of this I know is true,
One that came and changed my life, my love you know was you.

When the map of life had been mislaid, with no signpost to see,
Although I didn't know at once, you came to direct me.

You held my hand so gently and guided me so well,
Standing right behind me, to protect me if I fell.

Angels love is soft to touch, it keeps you safe and warm,
No need to see those angel wings, I know your shape and form.

Many problems we've encountered in parts of life's array,
But you've always been beside me, to help me through each day.

Life has not been easy, many mountains for to climb,
Together we have journeyed, and you've always had the time.

So when you think of angels, with wings and halo bright,
With cherub face and curly hair, wrapped in a gown of white.

Not all angels are in Heaven, some are sent to care,
It's a feeling that comes over you, when you realise they're there.

These angels are so beautiful, perfect works of art,
Real angels are the ones that touch the feelings in your heart.

Betty Hattersley (Tamworth)

Hopes And Dreams

People's lives are full of dreams
Few come true but yet it seems
That hope is always in our heart
To live and love until we part
Who knows what future has in store
Accept each day as the one before
As this occurs and times goes by
We all grow but never die.
Because our dreams just stay alive
To pass to others who will survive
So dream and hope for evermore
Life is for living and to adore.

Dorothy Haywood (Kingswinford)

The Rainbow

What do the colours mean to you?
The red and green and yellow and blue.
Think of a blue sky, and a yellow sun,
Shining brightly for everyone.

The life giving trees and grass so green,
That keeps our air so fresh and clean.
Golden corn grows to keep us fed,
And gives us all or daily bread.

The flowers that bloom their colours delight,
To lift us up from morn till night.
From reds and greens to purples and blues,
A rainbow of colour for me and you.

So when you're feeling sad and blue,
And the whole of the world seems to pick on you.
Remember behind that cloudy sky,
A rainbow is hiding for you nearby.

Margaret Hedley (Leeds)

True Love

Now never will we ever do
The many things we said;
For you left me in the early hours
Fast asleep in bed.
I still dream of things we used to say,
With you lying by my side
Like the time you said you loved me
And I walked along with pride,
But time is no real healer
For matters of the heart;
Because feelings can grow stronger
When it is true love from the start.

John Hickman (Kempsey)

I Am A Landmine

I'm a landmine
Without a mind
Hidden beneath the soil
Primed to explode, maim and kill
Waiting patiently for the patter of feet
To trigger the explosives packed within neat
Millions have died and suffered from my evil destruction
Governments continue to pay millions for this terrible invention
Have they no conscience to the misery and suffering they unleash?
Why not ban them from production, governments have banned
Lethal gasses?
As well as other destructive bombs to prevent generations from
Continual suffering.
Make a stand, force governments to respond in positive action,
Not bury their heads.
Cause them to have a conscience by forming marches demanding
They ban the bomb.
Demand action to breathe life into mostly third world societies
Not continual devastation!

Cecilia Hill (Stoke-on-Trent)

A Mother's Love

A mother's love is a wonderful thing
So strong and tender and true,
No matter what happens
She still thinks the best of you.

She does not ask for anything
She does not want a lot
All she needs is an hour or two
Of some of the time you've got.

As she sits there old and lonely
Thinking about you all
Wondering where you are today
Expecting you to call.

So spare an hour now and then
She does not ask for more
And see her sad old face light up
When you walk in the door.

She is just a grand old lady
Who has no claim to fame
Although you sometimes disagree
She loves you just the same.

But there's one thing that is certain
When she climbs that golden stair
There will be a great big welcome waiting
With our Lord and His angels there.

Eric Holmes (Doncaster)

Unease

I feel that I can't hold onto you
I know that I want to,
All I think about is you
Do you feel it too?

I watched you all day,
I could see your unease,
And how I was so pleased.

You feel threatened and hurt,
You're restricted to what you do
I can feel it too.
You'll never ever see me,
But I will always see you
No matter what you do.

I will be watching you.

Natalie Hudspeth (Retford)

The Great Divide Is Not So Wide - To Me

The great divide is not so wide
When loved ones are there and wait for you.
I almost see them as I look across
Crying out, 'I'm coming too!'
So tired right now and feeling weak,
Just anxious to go home.
To those who truly love me,
And never left me all alone.
Over there is Truth and Love,
'Tis where I long to be.
Away from a world that's getting darker,
Where many cannot see.
I am excluded from society
Cos I march to the beat of a different drum
So ostracised from their company,
And thus I am struck dumb.
With those who truly love me
I never say a word.
We communicate with tenderness
And every thought is heard.
'Tis why I feel I'm fading
Yearning for all that's true.
I see this world is dying
And I ache for a different view
'Twould be Heaven!

Rosie Hues (Birmingham)

This Man

Who is this man, this man invades my life
He is no woman's husband, and I am no man's wife.
Who is this man I ask you who roams within my soul,
He captures my attention, and then leaves a gaping hole.
Who is this man who fills my life and makes my heart beat faster,
I know without him life would be all chaos and disaster.
Who is this man who bides where men have stayed
And then moved on,
Ah yes, you may well ask my friend,
This man is my son.

M Huggett (Leeds)

It's Been

It's been a long time since I was here
If I had to think I would say a year
It's been a while since I could smile
Never been a time when it's been worthwhile
It's been a minute since I last cried
Wait a second, I'm still drying my eyes
It's been a long time since I have slept
Without them dreams that make me scared
It's been an hour since I last drank
The empty can still on the shelf
It's been five minutes since I last smoked
I have cut down . . . nobody thinks so
It's been three months since I last made myself sick
All I ever wanted was to stay a twig
It's not been a second since I wished I was dead
This thought is always lingering in my head
And if you asked me where I am
All I would reply is
I have a pair of scissors in my hand.

Stacey Hull (Ravenstone)

A Christmas Song

Watch the snowflakes falling
Hear the jingle bells calling
It's Merry Christmas today
It's Merry Christmas today.

Phones are busy ringing
Church choirs are singing
It's Merry Christmas today
It's Merry Christmas today.

Well wishers are meeting
Full of happiness greeting
It's Merry Christmas today
It's Merry Christmas today.

Jubilant people are dining
Decoration lights are shining
It's Merry Christmas today
It's Merry Christmas today.

Full of love, hearts are craving
And the world is raving
It's Merry Christmas today
It's Merry Christmas today.

Hamza Ismail (Luton)

An Old Man And His Dog

Have you seen an old man and his little dog?
You can see them walking, sometimes in the fog.
They go off in the morning, afternoon and night,
You can see them in the dark, or when it's light.

They'll be out strolling, even in the snow,
His dog is black but, it will guide him through.
Its walkies, walkies, many times during the day,
But the old man wouldn't like it any other way.

They've been together, nearly ten years now,
How calm this chap is, they rarely row.
The old man is quite nimble, although he's getting on,
We hope they have more walks, before he is gone.

The old man is caring and gentle to his little friend,
There must be a bond between them, we hope it doesn't end.
So if you're about and you see them here and there,
Give them a wave, say hello, show them that you care.

The old man won't forget his very good little friend,
Because his dog will be faithful, right to the end.
So if you have a dog, don't abandon it in the street,
Treat it like a human being, and it will wag its tail at your feet.

William Jebb (Stoke-on-Trent)

Fly Away

I wish I could fly like an eagle
Soaring away in the sky
Gliding and sweeping
Scanning below from on high.

I would leave all my troubles
Behind me
The worry of war here on earth
I would spread my wings
Fly away, and for peace and love
I would search.

If I had the wings of an eagle
The freedom to fly where I may
I would search the world
For beautiful places
Far away, far away.

Molly Kean (Leeds)

Thursday

I woke up this morning and shouted, 'Hooray
It's Thursday, it's Thursday, it's my massage day!'
Entering the room so pleasantly warm
To where the masseur awaits his skills to perform.
Aromatic oils pervading the air,
Expertly chosen blended with care.
Soft music playing like gurgling streams
Soothing my mind as I drift into dreams.
I feel so relaxed the world seems unreal,
Words cannot express the way that I feel.
Cascading waterfalls, sparkling sun,
A new day awaiting, life just begun.

Dorothy Kemp (Dunstable)

The Magic Of Spring

Yellow headed daffodils
Are dancing on the breeze.
Gathering pollen from them
Are the hairy bumblebees.
Jenny wrens are collecting moss
To line their nests so small,
And with the rising of the sun
Birds sing their tuneful call.
Weather is much warmer
With the lengthening of the days.
Green buds are appearing
And some trees have catkin sprays.
Fish have started feeding
Swimming round in local ponds.
Frogs are now emerging
Laying frogspawn in green fronds.
Spring has sprung at long last
And the sap is rising fast.
Nature's turned full circle
And her new spell has been cast.

Linda Knight (Belper)

Have You Ever

Have you ever loved someone who's meant so much to you?
Who filled your life with laughter and cared for you too?
Have you ever had your heart torn apart and broken into two?
If you've never had that feeling I pray you never do.
Have you ever made a wish you could turn back time,
So you could say all the things you didn't have time?
Have you ever felt so much heartache you can't face the day?
Or have shed a million teardrops that fall throughout the day?
Have you ever had your world turned upside down?
You feel so angry God has let you down.
Have you ever wished you had the chance to say goodbye
'Cause when lying in bed all you do is cry?
Have you ever looked up into the sky and asked God a million and
one times why?

I love you and will miss you so much Dave
RIP until we meet again
Love your cousin Maria

Maria Lambley (Nottingham)

The Blue-Tit Family

We are the garden acrobats,
Just watch us, the comic cuts!
Swinging on wires upside down,
Tackling all those nuts.
We wear such colourful costumes;
Bright blue jackets with yellow vests,
Bright blue caps upon our heads.
We're a cut above the rest!

We are extra light and agile,
On the thinnest twigs we can hang,
So we can select juicier buds
Than the rest of the Tit-Family gang.
We search window frames for spiders,
Just look for our bright yellow breasts,
Then you'll know it's the Blue-Tit Cleaners,
We're a cut above the rest!

There are others in our family;
Great, Willow, Marsh, Crested and Coal,
But we're the most intelligent,
Problem solving is our goal.
We peck the tops off milk bottles,
Gold top is always the best,
We adore the creamy stuff inside,
We're a cut above the rest!

We love to nest in old oak trees,
But sometimes we'll use a box.
We start pairing up in the New Year,
So much talent in our flocks!
We put all our eggs in one basket,
Producing one brood is a test.
They hatch when grubs are most plentiful.
We're a cut above the rest!

So don't forget to listen out
For our merry chirping call.
You'll see me, the wife and several kids
Sitting cheekily on your wall.
We'll train our chicks to perform the tricks
That you love to watch with glee,
And remember, the Blue-Tit troupe's
The best act you'll ever see!

Doreen Lawrence (Sandy)

Voyage

How often in the cool of evening
You would sit in the arbour sublime,
How often drift in your memory
In the gentle embrace of time.

How rare are the spirits that soften
In the mellow ripening of age;
Rarer still are the bearers of mercy
Whose forgiveness is writ on the page.

When love is a cruel tormentor
You would teach of her kinder traits,
And still in the confines of envy
Would you preach of her wider constraints.

How soon in life's sad, bitter journey
Are we forced to betray what is dear.
In the heat of the heart's tender giving
The absence of love is our fear.

So we travel to love's distant borders
Where even our souls wander free,
And passing through frontiers of needing,
Where once we were blind, we can see.

David Lea (Cheshire)

On Telling My Lady

Hope seems all but lost, barren and bare,
As I clutch a keepsake of my maiden fair -
She for whom my heart hath one plea;
In aching tears it begs 'love me . . .
Love me dear, for I love thee too;
This worn-down heart belongs to you.
A modest gift, and nought too fine,
Though regardless, yours, this heart of mine.'
But such wond'rous words she never could hear,
For telling such truths I truly do fear.
And being so cursed I weep in despair,
Clutching a keepsake of my maiden fair.

David Maidment (Coventry)

Tumbledown Cottage

Tumbledown cottage on the edge of the wood
Children can visit when they have been good
A large and magical place to see
Magic can happen quite constantly
Wizards hide in cupboards deep
All the dolls seem to sleep
Large lazy cobwebs hang from the roof
You must have to visit if you need more proof.

Jack-in-the-box is quiet tonight
If you touch him, he will jump alright
Trucks and cars all parked in a line
Waiting for a driver, oh, so fine!

It seems like a place that is quiet right now
At night it all comes to life somehow
When no one is ever around to see
What a lot of noise there must be.

If you could peep into the cottage unseen
You would know exactly what I mean
At night when the wizard waved his stick
They all jump to life, ever so quick
All the toys having a game on the floor
The mechanical spider climbing up the door
Trucks and cars racing all around
Even Jack-in-the-box can be found
Jumping out of his box on a spring
Having fun with everything

So when you visit tumbledown cottage
On the edge of the wood
Please make sure you have been good
Be very quiet and you just may see
All that has been long hidden from me.

G Mapes (Swindon)

My Children

A part of you I will always keep
Within my heart, locked in so deep
All my tomorrows, everything I do
Is sharing my life, with all of you.

Laughter and happiness, good times and bad
We will get through with the love we all have
To share with each other, a bond that's so strong
For being together, is where we belong.

You are my future so I can go on
In the years that follow, and when I am gone
So thank you my children,
For all that you've done
I'm so proud to say, that I am your mum.

Jacqueline Marriott (Watford)

Yobs' Anthem

We sit on our backsides
All day long.
Singing our anti social songs
We're not jerks, cos we won't work
We just hang around and collect all the perks
And let the smarties do it all.

A Marshall (Bedford)

Silent Plea

When I'm forgetful bear with me
    I know how frustrating it can be;
And when I can't hear what you say
    Don't treat me as if my mind is astray.
If my sight seems to be worse
    Don't get cross or inward curse -
Remember I can't help growing old
    Or feeling hot or then too cold!
The older one gets, the more one dreads
    The time when one seems to be losing the threads;
And blessed are they who strive to heed
    The silent calls of 'old age' need.

My needs are small, clear and free -
    Material things don't worry me.
A pleasant look, a surprise call,
    And understanding, that is all.
So don't think you must spend a lot
    Or be forever on the spot;
Just spare a little of your time
    Whilst you still enjoy your prime.
You'll find that God has much to give to
    Those who spread comfort while they live
And better still, you'll find it's true
    Your kindness will return to you.

Bessie Martin (Nr Selby)

On Our Golden Day

When you first walked into the room
All I could see was a rose in bloom
Your perfume seemed to fill the air
How pleased I was that I was there.

When I saw you my heart missed a beat
I could feel a tingling down to my feet
My mind was filled with thoughts divine
Oh how I wished you could be mine.

And when you turned and smiled at me,
My hopes quickly changed to reality.
It was then that my hopes were fired
Feeling my heart would get what I desired.

On the day we wed that dream came true
I really meant the vows I declared to you
That I would remember those vows I had taken
And that all others would be forsaken.

For fifty years a love we've shared
Our lives have shown how much we cared
The dreams I had when I first met you
Over the years have all come true.

And I can still see a rose in bloom
Whenever you walk into the room.

Ron Martin (Bulwell)

The Power Cut

Today we had a power cut
My kitchen was no good,
Of all the things I have in there
They won't work as they should,
I cannot boil myself an egg
Or make a cup of tea.
What would happen without power?
Is very plain to see.

Betty Mason (Dursley)

Thank You Mum

Oh! How I'd love to *say* to *you*
Mum . . . Happy Mother's Day
But sadly that's impossible
So I'd just like to say

Thank you Mum for all your love
Your discipline and care
Thank you Mum for helping me
And always being there.

I wish I'd said more often
Just how much I loved you so
But I took you for granted
And I always thought you'd know.

Yes you were my very best friend
One just like no other
And how I envy everyone
Who still have their lovely mother.

Jean Mason (Willenhall)

Poem

Here I sit within my chair
Watching the birds and the trees so tall
The flowers so lovely bed in my garden
And the grass so green for all to see
Oh I do wish you were here with me
To feed the birds and to laugh and sing
To walk in the sunlight and lay in my bed
Till the morning dawns.

S Mathers (Leeds)

Mane Nobiscum, Domine!

When evening spreads its shadows across the sky
And the darkness obliterates any light,
Lord, remain with us, within our sight.
At times we are afraid, filled with secret dread.
Joy vanishes like shooting stars if you are not here to share.
Living bread and prayer, give prisoners of conscience
Endurance under the torture,
This 'cruellest of animals' inflicts on them
To break with their spirit their will
And make them despair.
Inhuman power is still aborting, battering your flesh,
Failing to recognise you in the other.
You are the watershed between Heaven and Hell,
Providing the only love with the power to give life
And to consume all dross in the fire of the unifier.

Angela Matheson (Birmingham)

A Thousand Apologies

I'm sorry for all that I've done,
I'm sorry for causing such pain,
I'm sorry I lied, I'm sorry you cried,
I'm sorry it was all in vain.

I'm sorry for always being wrong,
I'm sorry for calling you names,
I'm sorry I made you feel guilty,
I'm sorry for all of those games.

I'm sorry for getting frustrated,
I'm sorry if you got scared,
I'm sorry I fell in love with you,
I'm sorry that I cared.

Itzhak Matthai (Cheltenham)

Your Love

I've gone through my life, I knew you were there
For all that I'm wanting is for someone to care
Now that I've listened to, seen, heard and touched
The thoughts of my mind didn't seem to feel much.

You've taught me a lot the short time I've known you
Your patience of an angel without feeling blue
Mention your name and I just seem to be
Calm and collected with a capital C.

Understanding and friendship with true love to boot
The soul of your being has given me root
To love someone back in the way that I do
Is to address their being and a love that is true.

I will always adore you for what you have done
You've made me see that I'm your only one
I will try to satisfy and make you feel proud
To show you my happiness to discard every cloud.

I love you now and forever and so much adore
The feelings you've given me are pleasant for sure
Always together that's the way we should stay
Without you here my darling I could not feel this way.

S Matthews (Nottingham)

Hospital Hell

Feeling so helpless, lost, alone,
They're all like zombies, one person, a clone.
The four walls are so white, sterile, so clean,
So cold looking, frightening, the floors even gleam.
The corridors are so long, daunting, endless,
I just want to go home, I want to end this,
Thinking of my bed, warm and snug,
All I want is a kiss and a big hug.
But back to reality and I'm closed in,
Buzzers going off, ring after ring.
Hoping I'll go home and get a decent night's sleep,
Thinking of home and the warm thoughts that I keep.

Melanie May (Worcester)

The Poppy Field

Norfolk fields are flat and green,
With hedges growing in-between.
Beside the roads ditches abound
With trickling water, a lovely sound.

We spy a field ablaze in red,
A field of poppies with glistening heads.
The poppies stand upright and bold,
They are a wonder to behold.
Harvested fields, stubble bare,
Hay rolls drying in the warm air.
Birds keep diving to the ground,
To see if any foods around.
As we gaze dreamily
We think how lucky, we are free.

Hazel McNeil (Northampton)

One Wish

I've searched almost everywhere
Still I can't find her
That special girl I can call mine
I know somewhere she's out there.

If I had one wish that came true
I know what that wish would be
To be with someone who loves me.

Maybe I found her but didn't know
I must have hurt her so badly
To make her want to go
Love is blind, you just can't see.

Sorry doesn't always make it right
For don't know what you've got till it's gone
Now I keep wishing every night
I was with that special one.

Love comes from out of the blue
Call it chance or call it fate
You're never too old so it's never too late
There's always someone out there for you.

Michael McNulty (Runcorn)

Life, Love And Learning

How many loves have I yet known?
Precious memories flooding back.
Most passions fade, indeed have flown,
But there's one that hasn't changed tack.

A chord struck on love's first morning
Going straightaway back to childhood,
Just as consciousness was dawning,
Unlike dreams that vanish for good.

Growing together without fuss,
Roaming over woodlands and fields,
Nature revealed herself to us,
In these formative years she yields.

This knowledge we hid from ourselves
We had stumbled on unaware,
Vision of truth and faith that delves,
These are the treasures that we share.

Sooner or later childhood passed
On entering the adult world,
Life's insights safely stored at last,
Labyrinths of the mind unfurled.

Gifts to receive, or be given,
Finding love was all around me,
Ever flowing like a river,
To the open arms of the sea.

Later in life, remembering
Childhood's early intimation,
Of love alighting on the wing,
Joy of action, not evasion.

Betty Mealand (Worcester)

Woman

With bodies bare
And long blonde hair
Young women of today
Live their lives happily
In their own way.

They still have homes and families
But cope in a modern way
Putting toddlers in nursery school
And leaving them there all day.

Life is not always easy
For the modern mum
But she struggles on
Doing her best
With very little time to rest
Sometimes promotion comes her way
Which of course means extra pay.

As time goes by
Those toddlers grow up
And become young women of today
Always remembering the example set
By their modern mum
They will never forget.

I Millington (Market Drayton)

This Is The Place That Love Calls Home

Head bent down with shoulders bowed
Too many burdens over the years
A husband, a father the roles he has played
Buried in work to escape one's fears
Babes in arms, adults now grown
A family around him yet so alone
The sleepless nights and aching pain
A mind that's turned near insane
All these feelings he's had to hide
Worn the mask to protect his pride
Strong for all but who's there for him
No one sees the truth within
Escapes into a forgotten world
Walks for miles in solitude
The wind on his face is freedom bound
Nothing but the distant sound
Of voices talking in his head
He asks for answers
But nothing's said
Love has left a bitter taste
All have taken without a trace
Will true love ever knock on the door?
Bring the one he's searching for
Maybe she's been there all the time
Just too scared to cross the line
But when he reaches to touch her hand
Finally he will understand
This is the place that love calls home.

Lisa Mills (Wolverhampton)

Trying To Be Patient

I've had my breakfast early,
Assorted biscuits for me,
Mum and Dad had a boiled egg a piece,
Buttered toast, and a hot cup of tea.

But what I find so boring,
Why must they just sit and talk?
Is it apple tree lane or the park today?
Oh I do want to go for my walk.

I've sprawled on the carpet, head between paws,
Tried to look nonchalant
I do really try to be patient at times
But it's a blooming long walk I want.

Well I do my best to do what dogs do,
Look cheesed off and give a big sigh
Why didn't God give doggies patience
Can He see how much I do try.

Oh Dad I'm fed up of waiting,
You've had your third cup of tea,
So I nuzzle my nose 'neath your elbow, 'Come on'
Oh it sure is a dog's life for me.

Dorothy M Mitchell (Evesham)

Somnambulance

Somnambulance, mild, brings to mine ear
Some dirging, young, cuckoo, sleepy yet clear,
Transpiring the faded, wafting dull shade
Of a twilight, verdure, meadow and glade.

I feel the pale roseate gleam of spring's dawn,
Warm on the bending petal:
It swings between the green, sharp spaces of serrated leaves:
I sense the wonder with breath bated.

Here is a king's love, a towering grace bestowed
On the deepest knowledge,
A place to hold in awe, serenity, release,
For tender longevity, tender peace.

Edmund Mooney (Birmingham)

O Silver Moon

I never heard a nightingale
Until I heard you sing,
A song of unrequited love,
Tied notes like knotted string.

No mortal could reprise that sound,
An angel might resign
His wings and choose to stay earthbound
For such a sweet repine.

Chanticleer salutes each dawning,
You serenade at dusk,
Day's requiem, a mourning,
Rose petals steeped in musk.

From vespers through to matins,
You trill the night away.
Does the moon, that old enchantress,
Hold you in her sway?

Jose Morgan (Derby)

The Price

Hours spent waiting
Senses screaming
A head that aches
From hopeless dreaming
A heart that's dying
From the pain
Of days and nights
Spent all in vain.
But who will notice
Who will care
Whose heart will break
When I'm not there?

B Morris (Luton)

Life Of The Leaf

Colouring the seasons up and down,
And all around with green, red and brown,
On the end of the fingers of trees,
We dance together in the breeze,
Going to and fro, always in a flap and a flutter,
Whilst on the ground we block the gutter,
Back to the soil which gave us birth,
Decomposing upon nature's earth.
During the seasons of summer and spring,
We suckle upon the light the sun does bring,
Giving our grand mother tree,
Some of Mother Nature's energy,
Absorbing her warm and loving kiss,
Whilst giving you oxygen from photosynthesis,
For you see the air that you breathe,
Is our gift to you, which you gladly receive.
Once we've died and settled upon the grass,
Where the wind did come to pass,
You show us great respect,
By bending knee in genuflect,
With a broom or rake in hand,
You return us to the soil and sand,
So once again we can feed,
Our mother tree, so she can seed,
And give birth to the next generation,
Of leaves, who then dance in life's celebration.

Dale Mullock (Rugby)

Thoughts From Long Ago

It seems not long ago, when small feet pattered round.
When joyful squeals of laughter were the only sounds.
But like it does, time passed me by, and into adults children grew.
Not quite the same, the laughter.
No more childish squeals of joy.
Our life has ways of showing us how worthwhile we can be.
My children now have children, these blessings I can see.
I watch while small feet patter round, and hear the sounds of joy.
It's all the same, it seems to me, just like long ago . . .

Jean Mulroy (Hayes)

Lost Love

The way I feel is so unreal
The way of life is sad
We choose our paths with bends and turns
But my heart forever yearns
For a love I thought I had.

It seems an age of endless time
Since in his arms I lay
But wish I may and wish I will
For every single day.

Try as I might to forget those nights
They live within me still
But he says there is no coming back
For in his love there is a lack
Of need for me for what I am.

A woman with love to give
Gentle as a lamb
But wish I may and wish I will
For every single day.

Kathryn Needham (Lowdham)

Looking Ahead

As I lay in the bed and think of my life
Another day I face with life's toil and strife
Wondering when this journey would end
Crying and groaning is my constant friend.

To cheer me up the radio I put on
Then heard the tragic news
Which left me withdrawn
A mother in a tragic crash
Had lost her life in an instant flash.

I reflect once more on my life
And thank God for dealing with my strife
I can walk.
I can talk
I can give my kids a meal.
Although I don't know when my end will come
My maker
Has given me a deal to rely on.

The moon and stars will forever shine
Looking at creation, can pass the time.
Any groans
Will be a delightful burst
Any tears shed
Will be a greeting
So no more talking about this life
Keep looking ahead
Walk to the light
It always gives direction
And eases my situation.

Angela Nevo Hopkins (Rubery)

Only You!

Take me to Paris, take me to Milan!
Take me anywhere, you know you are my only man.
I don't need things like big diamond rings,
Just say you love me and I'll feel like a queen!
Buy me flowers and chocolates too
You know there's no other like you!
So what I'm trying to say . . . *I only need you!*

I want you to know how I feel and love you so!
13 years old, and thought she knew all there was to know.
You lifted me up and asked me to be your girl,
My head began to whirl.
You should have seen me when I got home,
All loved up and could not sleep, my heart missed a beat.
So each time you lift me up, those feelings come flooding back,
And I still feel like that little girl!
Who loved you all those years ago!

Rose O'Connor (Orpington)

Shangri-La

The valley that I'm seeking,
Is one I seek alone,
The valley that I'm seeking,
Is moist and overgrown,
This valley that I'm seeking,
Can only be entered by a king,
To enter into this valley,
Will cost a Golden Ring.

Graham O'Gallear aka 'Fuzz' (Cannock)

Love Yourselves . . .

You are unique
As the sky
As every blade of grass . . .

If we can marvel at sun sprites on water
Or a perfect rose,
In that true moment of wholeness
Before petals fall,
If we rejoice in spring rain
Or winter snow,
An artist's picture
A poet's verse,
A friend's hug
Or a lady bug
Then surely we can learn
To love ourselves just a little bit.
Like a bird trying to fly
Or a baby's faltering steps.
OK! If love is too strong a word!
Then tonight just pretend
Let's start with like . . .
Go outside or just look through the curtain.
All those stars . . .
Maybe the moon.
Imagine you're at the first quarter
Aiming to be a full moon!
Big and shiny and new.
You are unique . . .
You have a name . . .
And you are worth loving too.

E Osmond (Nottingham)

The Path

Take a step in another direction
Doesn't matter how far or how slow
Reach out and you'll get there
Wherever you're destined to go
Release the heaviest of bundles
Cast aside all shadows and doubts
There's always time, a place and a reason
To discover what you're wanting to find out.

So ride the varied ripples
Surf high on the stormiest sea
This could be the journey
That's meant to set you free
So it doesn't really matter
Whether the path twists or just bends
The key is how you get there
And not how it ends.

Katherine Parker (Wolverhampton)

Not Just An Email

I am just a name, an icon on the screen.
I am small and do nothing more,
Yet I am seen by millions and used by more.
I bring you everything.
Sometimes slow but I deliver it all.
From news to letters,
From cards to messages,
From spam to information.

Yet I have no ambition,
Only you know what,
To send those special words,
From here to the heart.
I am here and can go wherever you wish.
Just type those three words,
And it will make a heart pound with joy.

I may be an icon,
I may deliver more of what you don't want,
I can connect you to whoever you want.
You may use me for many things.
But I'm quicker and better.
For three words I will send.

So send them an email
And put a smile on their face.

Paul Parkin (Ilkeston)

Daffodils

The Ides of March are scarce a week gone by
As by a Salop stream my steps are led,
And there ten thousand daffodils are spread
Their golden kisses blown toward the sky;
There seems no footage anywhere to tread
That is not by the new spring's bounty fed
On gold and orange, rising from the bed
Of last year's stricken leaves of empty dead,
As swathe on swathe into the wood they lie
Long since matured before the migrants come
To sing their happy songs, glad to be home;
The bitter winds of March they all defy
Unseen by any save the passer-by -
Or maybe by the Moon-God's tearful eye.

John Peaston (Blakedown)

Oh Not Valentine's Day Again?

We've never had time to be soppy
No room for chocolates or fizz
Our children we hoped wouldn't copy
But be famous somewhere in showbiz.

Hearts and flowers are always wasted
We don't go out for dinner
For food that should be just tasted
Eventually we must get thinner.

So now we've had a makeover
We're going to get blotto
Although the kids might take over
If we win the lotto.

How then could we be romantic?
Before we burst our bubble
Spoilt by someone quite pedantic
So instead we'll keep out of trouble.

You can keep all the glitz and hype
A romantic cruise on the QE2
To us it's a load of old tripe
We might have to take the kids too.

When the kids all leave home
But then I might have guessed
We'll have more under our little dome
Look how well we've been blessed.

Pauline Pickin (Wetherby)

Teenage Love

Teenage love,
Heart beating,
I don't know what to do,
Can't help these feelings, I'm getting over you.
I want to say 'I love you',
I want to kiss your lips,
I want you to know I'm there and I want to holds your hips.
Can't tell you how I'm feeling,
Don't want to let you know,
Don't know what is happening especially down below.
But every time I see you,
I feel a tingle deep inside,
Then panic overcomes me and I quickly run and hide.
So many secrets,
I try to play it cool,
Teenage love is tough love, especially at school.

Tony Pratt (Northampton)

The Somme

The 1st of July 1916 a bright day is dawning,
So different from the previous week of summer storms
And rain that was pouring.
Death came to many whose youth and blood was lost one summer's
day so early in the morning.
This place of hell and mud and death,
The smell of which was strong,
This awful place where our youth died,
The nightmarish bloody Somme.
The picket wire and no-man's-land,
The deafening sound of shells,
Signalled too many a man the sound of Heaven's bells.
Lined up in all those trenches,
The cream of Britain's crop,
Waiting for the signal to go over the top.
Row on row of men so neat soon to be sythed down within minutes
Like summer's billowing wheat.
The clatter of machine gunfire was the last thing most men heard
As they hurtled into no man's land and that sticky boggy earth.
Many lay upon the battlefield until their bodies were rotten,
But to me these brave and honourable men will never be forgotten.

Christopher Price (Coventry)

For David

Two years ago, or thereabouts,
We'd only heard your name,
But now we know and love you
Our lives aren't quite the same.
You made us very welcome
And took us out for dinner,
We're both very pleased to say
Gillian has picked a winner.

Irene Price (Allenton)

Field Of Grass

Walking through a field of grass,
On a summer Sunday morn,
Dewy blades between my toes,
I stand in awe at a new day born.

The sun rises over the hills,
Turns everything gold and green,
I breathe blossom-scented air,
No better place have I ever been.

My skin tingles with the heat,
The birds soar to greet the sun,
And trees stretch to touch the sky,
I feel man and nature become one.

Michelle Rae (Corby)

Snowbird

Gentle, lowly, silver-sweet
You're a snowbird, double feat:
Grace-defined and beauty too
None could ever compare to you.

Snow-white dove, you're fun to know
Ever bright and never low -
Bought such sunshine, stars and tears
Down my path, and calmed my fears.

Dear Selina, thou art dear -
Having brought your starlight near.
Burning candle, you're a star
Glistening golden rays hence far.

Coming at a time of woe
Shining spark and spirit, glow -
Fellow swan, some special sis'
Knowing you has been such bliss.

Kiran Rana (Littleover)

Springtime

I see the wind change, I see the sunshine come,
I see thousands of daffodils where I used to run.
I see lambs jumping, I see rabbits running, I see catkins swaying
In the breeze,
I see smiling faces, children playing and buds coming
On the trees.

I see fresh water streams and new life beginning,
I see love in the air that's clean,
I see the washing blowing,
I see Mum spring cleaning,
I see tea being late for me.

I see the ice melting, I see the young birds calling,
I see hope and better days to come,
I see lovers holding hands
And making their plans,
Like a new world has just begun.

I see my brother digging,
I see my new grandchild coming,
I see light at the end of the day,
I see winter's going back where it came
And I'm all happy again.

Madeline Reade (Swindon)

Shadows

Shadows flickering in the sun.
Shadows dancing, having fun.
Shadows fat and shadows small.
Shadows thin and very tall.
Shadows to the left and shadows to the right.
Shadows in the distance almost out of sight.
Shadows from the moonbeams.
Shadows from the sun.
Shadows playing funny tricks on each and every one.
Shadows across the waters.
Shadows across the skies.
Shadows across the landscapes.
Shadows before our eyes.
Shadows for the present.
Shadows from the past.
Shadows from our childhood.
Shadows of memories held fast.
Cast away those everyday shadows,
That are filled with darkness and doubt.
Let the light of God within your heart
And push the darkness out.
Remember! with every shadow
There is always hope in sight.
For you will never find a shadow
Without a ray of light.

Teressa Rhoden (Bilston)

Oh To Be Parents

'Oh' what worries kids do cause
No minutes to spare, no stops, no pause.
'Hip hoorah' for mams and dads
They nurture the lasses and the lads.

Sleepless nights with babes so small
Bottles, nappies, winding and all.
Concerns over illness, injections too,
Parents deserve medals, isn't it true?

Now kids are toddling, into mischief
Can't turn your back not even in brief.
Chasing them round, like a cat on hot bricks,
No wonder time moves on, double quick.

They're in their teens, you worry about crime
Off to university, away from home first time.
Think! Parents can relax, have time for each other,
'Oh' no such luck, sleepless nights not over.

'Ah' got their degrees, at last a good job,
They want to get wed, to a super heart-throb.
You warned them of parenthood, the good and bad,
Oh dear! They are soon to be
    A mam and a dad!

Carol Richmond (Leeds)

Robin Hood

Robin Hood fact or fiction
Sherwood Forest his jurisdiction
He robbed from the rich to give to the poor
A local legend that's for sure.

King Richard away fighting the crusades
Prince John in charge along with his aides
Double the taxes and make them pay
No! Not next week I mean today.

Subject who can't meet the new demands
Will suffer by his Lordship's hands
Pay up or else you know the threat
The new demands will be met.

Robin of Locksley, one who would not pay
Turned the tables that fateful day
He retreated to the forest with his bow
The prince and the sheriff he would show.

As dignitaries passed through the heather
Robberies took place whatever the weather
Reporting back to Nottingham Castle
The sheriff could do without the hassle.

The prince offered an handsome reward
But against Robin no one lifted a sword
Over the years his following grew
The locals stood by this man they knew.

A band of men dressed in Lincoln green
Blended into the forest not to be seen
Led by a man who lives in the wood
Locals refer to him as Robin Hood.

As the years passed by Robin laid down his head
Little John and Maid Marian at the side of his bed
Please pass me my bow and a single shot
Where the arrow lands will be my plot.

King Richard heard of this man's plight
Declaring that his cause was right
Sherwood Forest his jurisdiction
Robin Hood fact or fiction.

W Rodgers (Lonnie) (Worksop)

Born To Live

I was born to live,
Born to love,
Born to reach for the stars up above.

Born to live,
Never to die,
Born to laugh, but never to cry.

Born to love,
With all my soul,
Born to burn with a passion,
Like I've never known.

I was born to live,
Born to love,
In this life we were born to share,
Born to see the love in each other's eyes,
Born to live, born to love, born to care.

Pete Robins (Chesterfield)

Christmas

So many things please me at Christmas,
Things that money can't buy,
Cold, icy nights frosted with stars,
Orion riding the sky.

Tall, leafless trees and red sunsets,
Blue twilights, lamps in the mist.
Drawn curtains, tea by the fire,
Tackling the Christmas card list.

The thrill of the first Advent candle,
That one, tiny flickering ray.
Opening the calendar windows
To a new little picture each day.

Yet, it's good to send gifts out with love,
To put stars into small children's eyes.
To keep the sweet traditions of Christmas -
Create some wonder, surprise.

And so, 'the days are accomplished'
In the deep hush of Christmas Eve,
When His world is quietly waiting,
He comes - we believe!

Betty Rollitt (Doncaster)

Dreams

A dream wanders round in the circle of your mind
Leaving all cares and doubt behind,
Floating around on a snowy cloud
Happiness and gaiety knows no bounds.
The loved ones that you may have lost
Can appear in a dream as you turn and toss,
They speak - and you seem to hear
Only because they are so very dear.
So when you from a dream awake,
Keep the memories with you, never to forsake.

Sheila Ryan (St Albans)

The Bubble And The Reality Of Fashion

From catwalk to the celebrity magazines around today,
Women are made to look a certain way.
Models and famous women that weigh less pounds on the scale,
Attractive is beginning to look frail.

Women should not forget that fancy diets and surgery can be trouble.

As we women must enjoy our shape,
Size should not affect,
Let's take a moment to reflect,
Leave the fashion magazines behind
Think of all the positive things in mind.

What is the bubble and what is the reality of fashion?

Be confident and stand proud,
You are, who you are, and that's allowed!

J K Sahota

Clouds

Clouds ethereal . . . clouds sublime . . .
Clouds like snowy mountain ranges
Wisps of cloud that trail the sky
Like silky threads unravelling
Fleecy clouds and quilted clouds
Clouds that fly before the wind
Clouds like puffballs scarcely moving
Some that billow like an ocean
Stormy clouds and clashing clouds
Clouds with angry fists of thunder
Sunset clouds that seem on fire
Clouds of silver with the morning
And clouds . . . and clouds . . . and clouds . . .

E Scott (Birmingham)

My Love

I hold my love in my hands
I hold my love in my heart
My love's spilling over there's lots and lots
But now that we are apart
Where can I put it?
Where can it go?

I'll have to continue to hold it
Until one day when we die
You will feel it and take it with you
As your soul floats away past the sky
And then you will know how much I loved you.

Janet Scrivens (Leicester)

Mum

Right from when I was born
You meant the world to me
You're the twinkle in my eye
You're the sugar in my tea.

You gave me a home
I'd never swap you for any other
I'd never let you go
I love you so much mother.

You gave me hugs and kisses
When I was sad and down
When you are sat right next to me
I feel so safe and sound.

The world is now a happy place
Outside the skies are blue
Guess what - it's cause you're my mum
Remember I love you.

David Sheasby (Daventry)

Never Withers, Wanders, Worries

-     that cherished charge of mine
Lives so far,
Loves so deeply
Never misses a trick
Of wonder - great.
Supreme, superb
Always listens.
Always loves.
Never hates - never loves
Always here, there, everywhere.
Above the trees -
Settled in breeze -
Around about, within, below
Surrounding folk with wall so thick.
Wanders over hills with stick
Watching sheep; that's us, of course
Counting each and everyone.
Chatting cheerily and then clouds
Dim and gone, back to Heaven
From whence he wandered
Still watching, wondering, waiting -
Always full of love,
Arms outstretched over us all.
Never excludes one, wider arms than man.
Bigger eyes,
Bigger heart,
Just Jesus.

Jac Simmons (Northampton)

It's Over

My eyes are burning for your love is turning,
I'm no longer the girl of your dreams.
My stomach's churning and I'll keep on yearning,
Nothing is what it seems.

My heart is hurting, are you doing the dirty,
My smile has gone from my face.
My life is crashing, I'll keep on asking,
Why you needed so much space.

My tears are streaming, I know I'm not dreaming,
That my life has turned upside down.
My heart was beating yet yours wasn't speaking,
And now you're no longer around.

My body's shaking as we're no longer dating,
My heart is snapping in two.
No need to be faking, I know yours is not breaking,
Oh how I wish this wasn't true.

You gave the excuses, I gave the abuses,
Because I'm hurting more than you know.
Is this what your choice is, we'll share no more noises,
I really wish this wasn't so.

You kept disappearing; this was what I was fearing,
You just left me on my own,
I'll no longer be hearing the voice of your cheering,
Just the echo of the dialling tone.

I saw you as my clover, but now we are over,
Luck is no longer on my side.
You were my lover, but did you have some other,
I questioned after you had lied.

You gave me no answers, as I kept giving more chances,
So now you can start anew.
I hope you are now happy, cause with me you were unhappy,
So now I say goodbye to you.

Gemma Smith (Nottingham)

Wonderment

My heart is yearning,
Also emotions churning.
All actions defeat me.
With only you on my mind completely.
The whole of my love
Flows towards only you,
Full of fondness and vigour
I cannot withhold.
If your love was a rainbow
I'd seal it with gold.
Please feel the same way
And we'll journey to the coast,
Wandering hand in hand along the bay.
Sharing one another's thoughts,
Happiness and joy along the way
How I wish you were my valentine.

Paul Smith (Worcester)

I Hear The Leaves Echo

Once in a while
Echoes whistles
In the thistles
Aura's of the old and gone
Something has begun
Handed down prams
To go on with true grit
Mom often has to sit
A leaf out of a book
Soaring higher and look
Another brand new day
People naturally weep
Best not to go too deep
A lot of concentration and less sleep
Too weak to speak
Think less and see what you reap
Like a housemartin or a swift
A heavy burden will drift
For to err is nature
And nature is God's gift.

Hardeep Singh-Leader (Leicester)

Tread Softly

Tread softly on my dreams
Of imaginative thought.
Tread softly on my dreams
So soft -
Yet strong with iron wrought.

Tread softly on the human love
Sincere in every way
Tread softly on maternal thoughts
That enfold you
Each new day.

Tread softly on my dreams
Each night
When I picture your
Dear face -
Tread softly - draw me to
Your breast
For my maternal kiss.
Tread softly.

Mary Skelton (Nottingham)

Seventh Day Of The Week

So many stories from around the world
How the Earth was made.
The Creator God,
I like!
Does this make me Muslim, Christian or Jew?

With the rules drawn out in the sand
We define our beliefs.
God's rest day,
I like!
Sunday is the last day of the week?
I must be a Jew?

Will the only mouth be that of a gun?
Hatred, inflamed again?
The one God,
I like!
The last day, the first day?
Which prophet's words bring us to prayer?
Does it really matter?
I must be a heretic!

Let's start fighting;
We always have and
I suppose,
We always will.

Barbara Sommer (Salop)

Heathland

Golden gorse, bright purple heather,
On the heath under summer skies.
Tall grasses, birds and wild flowers,
A melody when the skylark flies.

The trees seen in the distance,
Many years they have stood.
Their paths seem dark and mysterious,
Leading the way through the wood.

There's a beady-eyed black crow,
Framed in a silver birch tree.
Most disgruntled on his lofty perch,
He seems to be looking at me.

There are brambles and many butterflies,
Lots of insects are busy too.
So are the rabbits hopping around,
They have all of this grass to chew.

On dazzling blue fluorescent wings,
A dragonfly hovers and dashes,
Amongst the yellow and purple,
Appear the blue and green flashes.

Over the heaths and heathers,
Cool water in the streams,
Nettles, brambles and wild flowers,
Watching, animals, birds, insects and trees.

Joan Hawkes (Birmingham)

Amazing

A mazing charisma, so bright it shines through
M agnificent personality, making me warm to you
A ctual beauty too real to see
Z ippy, mad and just like me
I ntelligent, witty and educated right through
N othing could stop me liking you
G orgeous too. What's wrong with you?

Gemma Steele (Birmingham)

The Pirate

You are looking for a shelter
Just to ride away the storm
But your cargo will be mine
I will not wait until the dawn
All your sails have been removed
You cannot put up a fight
And your fairy tale dreams
I may remove before the light.

I will take from you the dream
Of that one to make you whole
Show the naked truth of life
Bear that thing you call a soul
I will leave you floating helpless
With a heart no longer strong
Not so righteous or so proud
For the next to come along.

You have seen this flag before
Skull and crossbones I do fly
I expose to you the truth
Will not hide behind a lie
So don't turn to me tomorrow
Make believe this can't be so
For I will take what's there to give
I am a pirate don't you know.

Paul Stone (Birmingham)

Anniversary

Like the leaves of the vine
Intertwined with love
Their bond stands the test of time,
Like the bill and coo of the turtle dove,
Sweet harmony rules sublime,
Let us wish for them both
As they go on their way,
Carefree as the gentle moth,
A life full of joy, pleasure and fun -
A toast - to a wonderful day!

Valma Streatfield (Reading)

After The Bombs

After the bombs in London
After the grief and pain
After the fear, the speeches,
What's to stop it happening again?

Right Mr Politician
now who is incorrect?
Wrong Mr Politician
is my neighbour
a terrorist suspect?

Valerie Sutton (Nottingham)

Keep Only The Best

Put your worries in the rubbish bin
Smile, as the neighbours you meet
Leave grumbles behind, keep a merry heart
Make yours a happy street
Listen when others tell you their woes
Though you may have enough of your own
Bring hope to your future knowing God is near
Then find many of your troubles have flown.

Muriel Tate (Derby)

The Number One

We should love ourselves for there is only one,
Be true to ourselves before the time is gone,
Our true identity is hard to find,
It comes from the heart and deep in the mind,
A fear of change isn't so rare,
To be yourself if you dare,
Perfect loves drives out all fear,
We have lots of help from those dear,
I don't want to change these words are often thought,
We don't look at ourselves like we ought,
So love and care for the number one,
If you lose the smile still hold on.

Lisa Thompson (Doncaster)

Two Hearts

Our two hearts entwined
A love like ours so hard to find
Maybe once in a blue moon
Maybe once upon a lifetime.

Our love that binds so strong
A love that can't be wrong
A love so pure and true
Two hearts as one . . . that's me and you!

Our love that fate thrust upon us
My heart to you . . . I entrust
One moment in time that was meant to be
Two hearts entwined . . . our destiny!

Our hearts now they beat as one
Shine brightly as the midday sun
As bright as a star in heaven's above
Two hearts entwined . . . bound with love!

Lynn Thompson (Nuneaton)

Countryside Alliance

The fox was hunted, the stag was hunted
They snared the rabbit and coursed the hare
They frightened the pheasant into flight
And then blasted it out of the air!
The fox said, 'Enough! My fellow's wild
We need to unite in just cause!'
Then deep in thought he pondered a while
And after a ponderous pause . . .
'We must take our grievance to the 'City of Men'
In defence of all wild creatures!
It will be hazardous, dangerous, hard,
And against all that our instinct will teach us!'
So they started on foot through meadows and woods
At night so they wouldn't be seen
Gathering animals along the way
The mink were particularly keen!
Then came the morning the invasion they'd mount
In the distance they sighted 'Big Ben'
And so an army of animals too many to count
Entered the 'City of Men'.
They hopped over buses, galloped around cars
Stole the food from the hands of the drinkers in bars
And the city folk stood and gazed as in awe
As the fox bravely knocked on the Downing Street Door!
'Prime Minister Sir! We are here in defiance!
Our only home is the countryside
And we're the Alliance!

Marji Tomlinson (Tamworth)

Why?

Why are we here? What have we done?
To make this life such a thankless one.
This beautiful Earth that God gave with love
For all to enjoy should be free as a dove,
But with all the anger and fighting and killing
We're spoiling it all and no one seems willing.
To say 'That's enough, don't let's be greedy
Don't let's keep taking, let's give to the needy
Let's all help each other before it's too late
Don't expect everything free on a plate
Let's teach our children the real way to live
How to love, and how to give
If we love them and lead them
And show them what's right
They won't need to find drugs
And a bed for the night.'
Will it be done, I very much doubt
Until those in charge stand up and shout.
The future is yours, all you children out there
Please don't be selfish
Show us you care
It's up to us all not just one nation
And we'll change the whole world
In one generation.

Joy Toms (Cheltenham)

Choice

Choice is a word, we barely use
A word, we very rarely choose
We have a choice, in what we do,
To give advice, a point of view.

We choose our friends, and lovers too,
But limited in choice, there's just too few
Some choose to laugh, or even cry,
Others may stop and wonder why.

To choose to be jealous, love or hate
Choice in whom, we choose for a mate,
So listen everyone, hear my voice,
Don't hesitate, just make the right choice.

Choose to smile, and get along
Smile, once in a while, you won't go wrong
If you choose to be sad, I ask why,
Live life to the full, before you die.

Kay Tonks (Wolverhampton)

Raindrops Of Kisses

An angel's delight
Of friendship
So honest and pure
Showered with hugs
Raindrops of kisses
Bring warmth to the
Heart of a sheltered soul
Loneliness eroded by the
Gentle beauty of words
That are whispered against
The wind, slowly settling like
Fairy dust - that is the beauty
Of each new day
The love of a true and honest friend.

Samantha Vaughan (Aylesbury)

Starlight

The swirling silvery sky alive with stars
That take my breath away on this frosty night.
The sky is a dream and can't be touched by man,
Who doesn't know why,
The universe unfolds but cannot answer,
The dark deep questions
Of 'How?' or 'Why?'
Our Earth is swallowed by the velvety texture,
Of the night sky.
When the stars whisper.

Mary Wain (Loughborough)

Sports Day

The five year olds were first to go
One hundred yards, their race seemed slow,
The finish line was not their goal,
They turned and smiled and onward flew.
The race in sacks was oh such fun,
Who cared who won or who came last,
One race all stopped before the line,
They all came first by holding hands,
The headmaster thought it all was fun,
Then organised the teams in lines,
And like a captain of his ship,
Made sure the baton they all gripped.
The egg and spoon race was the best,
The one in front became the last.
The team relay the last to race,
Each year ran out at such a pace,
For Eagle, Hawk or Falcon's house.
Thy shouted, screamed, they did not pause,
All left the field their day was run,
Exhausted . . . changed, went home with Mum.

D M Walford (Cleobury Mortimer)

At The Start Of Term

The pupils sit before computers, surfing the Internet.
Whatever they are looking for they haven't found it yet.
The master stands redundant beside the blackboard there,
A square peg in a round hole or a round one in a square.
What would they be doing if term hadn't started as yet?
Sitting before the home computer, surfing the Internet.

Things were very different when I was just a lad -
No electronic aids; ready reckoners were considered bad.
The desks were arranged in rows, all facing to the front.
The form-master was a hefty guy; he could be very blunt.
We did our sums; arith, geom, alge, and trig.
(The math's master had a bald head under a bushy wig).
There were square roots, logarithms and hypotenuse
And umpteen other terms, young people to confuse.
We did English lit, French verbs and Latin declensions
And many other word forms, too numerous now to mention.
We did our weekly essays on subjects far and wide.
We did Geography and History; we took them in our stride.

Now where has all that got me as year on year rolls by
And here I am a pensioner, just queuing up to die?
Of one thing I'm quite certain - I'm not all set
To sit before a computer screen, surfing the Internet.
But still I have my own double-U, double-U, double-U.
Not 'World Wide Web' just 'Walton With Wife' t'you.

P Walton (Leek)

My Sad Poem

I will sit and write this poem
About how very sad I feel
All the grief I feel inside
It all seems so unreal
Life at this time seems hard to bear
My daughters are not friends
I love them both very much
My love will never end
At night before I go to sleep
It's always on my mind
Quite often I will have a little weep
I wish life could be more kind
I laugh and joke so good at pretending
That life is a game and I must play on
Like the broken-hearted clown his life in tatters
Has to go on with his act when all hope has gone
So I keep hoping each day through
For something that can never be
Until my last day comes around
There will be no peace for me.

May Ward (Leek)

Christmas Day

It's Christmas Day,
Santa and sleigh,
He's left some toys for the kids to play.
Yours and mine,
Our families join
To eat mince pies and drink mulled wine.
Each takes a seat,
Eats turkey meat,
Then Christmas pud, makes meal complete.
We rest till three,
Drink cup of tea,
Turn on the box, her Majesty.
Beneath the tree,
A gift for me
And each one in the family.
Without a care,
Kids paper tear,
Each wants to see just what's in there.
Grandad he's got socks,
Pink tie that shocks
Four handkerchiefs in fancy box.
For dear old nan,
Some spray in can.
Asks, 'Will the smell attract young man?'
Now evening meal,
Crackers reveal,
Plastic tat, paper hat, no appeal.
A time for play
And then away.
Oh did I say, 'It's Christ's birthday!'

Albert Watson (Birmingham)

Love Figures

Do you still love me as much today
And the woman I have become?
I know I've put on some weight
Since that day I became a mum.
But you're not that man I married
Gone is the tall, slim handsome guy
Who would take my breath away
With that special glint in his eye.
I'd like to be really slim again
With no tummy and tiny waist
Now it's buying clothes for comfort
And never too tightly laced.
You have lost a lot of hair now
Your tummy has certainly spread
We really need to get more exercise
Not use the car but our feet instead.
We vowed we'd always stay together
Through the bad times and the good
Let's accept ourselves the way we are
Perhaps cutting back a bit on the food.
It was love that brought us together
And it's love that will see us through
There's that bit more to cuddle these days
But I can still get my arms around you.

Judith Watts (Abbots Langley)

Angel Of Gold

Without you dear Mother we wouldn't be here
Without you our world would not be so clear
You've taught us that love is a life driving force
You've taught to forgive through each difficult course
You've shown us the light at the end of the dark
You've lit up our lives with the tiniest spark
You've taught us that right is much better than wrong
You've given us strength when we haven't been strong
You've taught us to laugh when we wanted to cry
You've shown us we'll win if we only will try
You've taught us to give even when we're without
And appreciate nature and what it's about
To take not for granted to question and ask
To summon up courage and conquer each task
You've taught us to take every day in our stride
And comfort the needy with arms open wide
You've taught us to trust and you've taught us to care
And carry on loving once she's in God's care
So now that God's saved her a place in his heart
We know that we'll never be that far apart
We'll still see her smile when we open our eyes
We'll still hear her laugh through our tears of goodbyes
We'll still have our memories to ponder and love
And to trust in our Lord in His heaven above
So He has an angel who's precious and kind
Who's now left her family and friends all behind
But God's been quite patient so it's His time to hold
Our mother, our lifeline, our angel of gold.

David Whitney (Wellingborough)

Together

I wish that you were here, love,
To share my life with me;
For we would have such fun, love:
So much happier time would be.

There'd be more joy in living,
With you, good times to share;
And even more joy giving,
With ideas to compare.

Life would be a pleasure -
Even humdrum chores to do -
If we could spend our leisure
And I, be close to you.

We'd find so much to talk about,
So many things to do;
So many places to explore,
Sharing pleasures new.

When times got somewhat harder,
With troubles in our lives,
We'd be there for one another,
Life's trials to survive.

For we could help each other,
And soften Life's hard blows;
In companionship, we'd smother
The loneliness that old age grows.

Oh, say you feel the same, love,
And we, our lives could merge.
Sharing one abode, love,
Our spirits to converge.

It is my dearest wish, love - in truth, the only one -
That we should be together until our days are done.

Bee Wickens (Chesterfield)

Why?

Why do we have turkey for dinner,
When half the world is getting thinner?
And Christmas pudding in the dish,
When half the world can only wish?
And candles, cards, cake and more,
When half the world is less than poor?

Why do we have a room to spare,
When Jesus was born and had nowhere?
Why was he born in a stable mean,
Instead of a palace for King and Queen?
Why in a rough wood manger lain
Born to share in a world of pain?

He knew how to live without a home
And what it is the streets to roam
To see mankind in all its mess
And feel its heartache, pain and stress.

Why not within our celebration fun
Remember Him God's only Son
And celebrate His gift of life
Who came to help us in our strife.
And as we do, what could we more,
Than pray and give to help the poor.

Colin Wide (Bristol)

Jade

Oh what a cat this feline can be
Purring and miaowing and rubbing on me
There in the morning when early I rise
She'll curl and she'll roll and then earn her prize
Of a tickle of ear and a rub of the tum
Then off up the stairs to my bed she will run
She'll curl on the pillow for all of the day
Come hail, rain or shine that's where she will stay
Then on my homecoming our Jade she will rise
With a yawn and a stretch and no sense of surprise
She'll deem to descend once more for a prize
And she'll eat of the fare be it wet or it dry
Though if she dislikes she will simply pass by
If the weather is fair to the garden she'll venture
But she's old and she's wise and it's no new adventure
For soon she'll return and without any care
She'll roll all around
Cover carpets with hair
The wife she will curse and holler and shout
But Jade takes no notice she just rolls about
Then in the evening of zest she is full
Curtains, carpets and cushions she'll pull
'Oh put out the cat,' my wife she will say
For though she's quite good
She is funny that way
But it's time to repose
And Jade seems to know
For she's under the table laid ever so low
So then through some coaxing and maybe deceit
She comes once again and curls at my feet
Then into my arms what a day she has led
You've had a hard day Jade
It's time for your bed.

M Wiggin (Stafford)

Joe Muggins

If life's a daily struggle,
And you're fed-up all the time,
Perhaps your worklife balance,
Is swinging out of line.
Maybe no satisfaction,
Is causing you distress,
And being took for granted,
Leaves you sorting out a mess.
Well here's a good solution,
If you're feeling all washed out,
Put your feet up, read the paper,
And lock the Blighters out!

M Wilcox (Aylesbury)

Friends

Friends splash our world with colour
Setting our hearts to flight
Offering us shelter from the storm
They turn our dark to light.
Friends are the water to our soul
That nourish and help us to grow
Enriching our lives by their presence
With all the love and care that they show
Friends help to blow away the storm clouds
Turning our dark skies to blue
They lift our hearts and inspire us
By the loving things they say and do
Friends make our world multicoloured
When they walk closely by our side
With words of hope and encouragement
And their arms which are stretched out wide.
Friends always affirm and accept us
They help us to recognise
The blessings we have before us
Viewing our troubles through different eyes
Friends have a very special way
To bring out the best in you
Offering love, care and support
In the trials, you are going through.
Friends play such an important role
That's why I really believe
To have a friend you need to be a friend
For what you give, you will also receive.

Karen Wilson (Doncaster)

Patient-Patient

It seems so many years ago, when I was very ill,
I thought my time was getting near, but I am here still.
They took me into hospital to have an operation,
I lay there feeling poorly, but with good anticipation.

I couldn't let the nurses down, I knew they'd done their best.
They'd tried to turn my life around, so I just tried to rest.
Friends and family standing by, not wanting me to see them cry,
So maybe if my time is near forgive me if I shed a tear.

I'll climb that stairway to the sky, there waiting here to say,
My 'Goodbye.'
My life has been a happy one, so now I'll be with Dad and Mum.

I met St Peter at the gate, He told me off for being late!
He then said, 'You're not listed here, it mustn't be your time my dear.'
They said it was not time for me, many were more worthier than me.
I truly thought, 'It's time to go,' it's often said, 'you never know.'

I found that staircase hard to climb, it might be easier sliding down.
It was so hard that final mile, but I know I will raise a smile.
It really was a struggle when they put me to the test,
Now I've been given one more chance, I'm going to try to do my best.

Jean Windle (Milton Keynes)

I Like Cats And Cats Like Me

I like cats and cats like me,
With their loving, pleasing personality.
Cats are pleasure on a miserable day -
Purring softly, gently soothing stress away . . .

A cat quietly licking at its fur,
Grooming mid a contented purr;
A touch of a paw on the knee,
Telling of the need of company . . .

Coming home to an empty house isn't fun -
Getting a cat is the best thing I have done
To veer off the loneliness of 'my' empty home,
Cats aren't like men - they rarely roam . . .

So, don't be alone -
Get a cat to call your own;
Stroke it and tend its every need,
And you will be comforted - yes indeed . . .

You will find joy beyond compare
In this sad world of great despair
If you put on your coat and put on your hat
And go out and get yourself a cat . . .

You can talk to and cuddle a cat,
And I can guarantee you that
In a loving environment of a 'caring' home
Your friend the cat won't want to roam . . .

Mary Winter, née Coleman (Market Harborough)

Morning Breaks

When daybreak splits the clouds at night
Such beauty then invades my sight
A picture painted clear and bold
With skies of blue, of pink and gold
And gentle breeze to fan the earth
Gives blessing then of so much worth
To share with each and every one
Till warming hours bring the sun
Then I awake and greet the morn
As a bright new day is born
Then on my knees I say a prayer
I ask God keep me in His care
Through dark of night
And morning's light
Dear Father - as each day should be
When in despair Lord - carry me.

Joan Winwood (Bridgnorth)

Every Time We Say Goodbye

Every time we say goodbye
Your journey's far
I can hear your cry
You do your job once more
I bid farewell
When you close that door.
Your heart is lonely
Your tears I taste
My tears for you
I have to wait
Hoping you will come
Back to me again
My body is aching
Alongside the rain,
I can feel your pain.
You go to war
To fight for freedom
You can see the people
You can hear, see and feel them,
Your buddies,
Are falling all around
Blood everywhere
Upon the ground,
Rifles shooting
Trucks blown up
You cry inside,
I've had a f***ing 'nough.
What's this all for?
I ask myself
This war will never end.
Poppies in remembrance
To everyone of them all,
Soldiers in combat
At your feet
Now, we fall.

Mary Woolvin (Oldbury)

With Hope Afresh

In the month of February, golden catkins sway
And we are rewarded again with a sunny day,
They cavort and prance in an early Spring breeze,
So gently exploring our stately, old cobnut trees
Where the blackbird reigns supreme, to warble sweet,
His most delightful song, to our ears, fabulous treat,
To rival the robin, whose fruitful garden he'll share
And come what may, they will always be there -
To await your return, all of us yearn.

Although you may not see all you held dear,
Yet you still know of the seasons every year,
And can feel a new warmth replace winter's cold,
Knowing dormant plants will soon thrive, take hold,
And give out their message thro' enriched soil,
As God intended and, only mankind can despoil,
But for now, summer's promise is not far away,
With its glorious portent - and so we all pray
For that happy boon, come back soon.

And then tiny snowdrops make known their presence,
Snowy white, charming, of Spring's very essence,
Clinging to banks, to hedgerows and deep woods,
Where bluebells and buttercups await aconite's hoods,
And we two shall walk, braving those country stiles -
With all our companions, we may still walk miles,
Returning, refreshed, though quite tired and worn,
To await the coming of yet another bright morn.
When you emerge, to cross that verge.

All our prayers have been said, our heart's spoken,
That you will come back to us, mended, unbroken.
To share in all those things so dear in your mind,
For surely God will spare you, He is so kind,
And will show us all, by His love, you are safe -
Soon to come home - we must keep our faith,
Believing that Springtime gives fresh hope anew,
In the palm of His hand, He holds me and you,
In His loving care - always there.

Julia Eva Yeardye (Chesham)

The 11th Hour

On this day
The 11th hour
Of the 11th day
Of the 11th month
We stand still and pray
To all that were killed
In all the wars
God bless them all
Each and everyone.

Ella Wright (Ilkeston)

Anchor Books Information

We hope you have enjoyed reading this book - and that you will continue to enjoy it in the coming years.

If you like reading and writing poetry drop us a line, or give us a call, and we'll send you a free information pack.

Alternatively if you would like to order further copies of this book or any of our other titles, then please give us a call or log onto our website at www.forwardpress.co.uk

**Anchor Books Information
Remus House
Coltsfoot Drive
Peterborough
PE2 9JX**

(01733) 898102